# *Brookline*
# *Allston-Brighton*
### AND THE RENEWAL
#### *of*
# *Boston*

# Brookline Allston-Brighton

## AND THE RENEWAL

### *of*

# Boston

TED CLARKE

THE
History
PRESS

Published by The History Press
Charleston, SC 29403
www.historypress.net

All images within this book are from Wikipedia.org, the author's collection and Damrellsfire.com.
*Front cover image:* Cornhill, Boston, 1962.
*Back cover images:* Frederick Law Olmsted National Historic Site, Brookline, Long Wharf and Boston's West End.

First published 2010

Manufactured in the United States

ISBN 978.1.60949.185.7

Clarke, Theodore G.
Brookline, Alston-Brighton, and the renewal of Boston / Ted Clarke.
p. cm.
Includes bibliographical references.
ISBN 978-1-60949-185-7
1. Urban renewal--Massachusetts--Boston--History. 2. Social change--Massachusetts-
-Boston--History. 3. Community life--Massachusetts--Boston--History. 4. Brookline
(Mass.)--Social conditions. 5. Brighton (Boston, Mass.)--Social conditions. 6. Brookline
(Mass.)--History. 7. Brighton (Boston, Mass.)--History. 8. Boston (Mass.)--Social conditions.
9. Boston (Mass.)--Politics and government. 10. Boston (Mass.)--History. I. Title.
HT177.B6C55 2010
307.3'4160974461--dc22
2010045558

*Notice*: The information in this book is true and complete to the best of our knowledge. It is offered without guarantee on the part of the author or The History Press. The author and The History Press disclaim all liability in connection with the use of this book.

# Contents

# *Introduction*

In the first half of the nineteenth century, Boston, with new confidence, built itself into the fourth-largest industrial city in the country. It reached that level by 1880. But it would hit its zenith shortly after that and go into a dreary decline.

Switching from a maritime to a manufacturing economy, filling in the Back Bay when land became scarce, solving traffic snarls by digging North America's first subway and establishing a cultural haven—these are all things that suggest forward thinking and a good deal of flexibility.

Brighton and Brookline, close to Boston and to each other, began to grow, especially as Boston became overly crowded. They grew mostly along the lines of public transportation that were built within them, but they grew at different rates and in different ways. In due time, they went their separate ways.

The town of Brighton became part of the city, while Brookline voted to remain separate for its own reasons. Each had its own distinct spurs to growth, and they continued to grow, both doing better than the downtown in the decades up through the Second World War. In the period following that, Brighton fell victim to the same loss of middle-class people to the suburbs as Boston did. Brookline, a suburb itself, had sustained growth through this same period.

By the early decades of the twentieth century, Boston was no longer a world-class city; it was a city in decline—a city in the doldrums. It showed no creative spark, no progress and little hope.

What happened? How does a place become mired in depression? What made all that bright hope vanish? And then, what happened to allow Boston to make a comeback? Who would lead its resurgence and how did they do it? This slim volume will tell you those things and more.

# Chapter I

# *Recovering from the Great Boston Fire*

By the time of the Great Boston Fire, November 9, 1872, Boston was beginning what others and I have called its first golden age. At that time, the Back Bay was unfinished, and most of the cultural institutions had yet to move there from downtown. But the fire would change all that.

The fire began on the corner of Summer and Kingston Streets, a block south of where Macy's stands today, and it spread rapidly. It took a long time for someone to use the call box and report it. In fact, the fire was seen from hilly Charlestown before it was reported. Ironically, fire alarm boxes were kept locked at that time in order to prevent false alarms. It took twenty minutes to get the key and call in the alarm from a nearby box.

Viewers from Charlestown had balcony seats as the bright, moonlit night made everything clearly visible, and the hot fire with its plumes of flame provided not only lighting to the scene but drama as well.

Locked call boxes weren't the only complication. Another difficulty is highlighted in many tellings of the story. An epidemic of horse flu had sidelined the animals that pulled the fire equipment, so it instead had to be hauled by volunteers on foot. Nonetheless, these men had been trained. They pulled with a will and were only somewhat slower than the horse-drawn teams would have been. Horse flu was but a sidebar to the main story.

Equipment moving at any speed might have been too slow since the fire spread quickly, particularly through the top floors of buildings—connected or near one another—where combustible materials were stored and where the wooden French mansard roofs often caught fire from flying embers. This problem was made more serious by the inability of the steam engine pumpers to draw sufficient water to reach the tops of tall buildings in the narrow streets, particularly Summer. That was because the six-inch pipes in this section of town were too narrow to provide enough pressure to project the water five stories high.

Gas lines were used for lighting within the buildings, and many of these burst into flame before they could be shut off. Postmaster William L. Burt, who would play a major role in fighting the fire, described what he witnessed: "I saw in the most intense part of the fire, huge bodies of gas; you might say 25 feet in diameter—dark opaque masses, combined with the gases from the pile of burning merchandise—rise 200 feet in the air and explode, shooting out large lines of flame fifty to sixty feet in every direction, with an explosion that was marked as the explosion of a bomb."

The fire was stopped at State Street by a brigade of firefighters with pumps, saving the Old State House for posterity. Also saved by extraordinary effort was the Old South Meetinghouse at Milk and Washington. Credit is given to a crew from Portsmouth, New Hampshire, who arrived by train with their steam engine, Kearsage No. 3, that had been loaded on a flatbed railroad car and hauled by train to Boston. Its crew hitched it to a hydrant and soaked the roof of the church with a steady stream, thereby saving it.

What became known as the Great Boston Fire took about twelve hours to contain. By that time it had destroyed about sixty-five acres in the business section of the city in an area between Summer, Washington and Milk Streets and the ocean. That included 776 buildings at a cost of nearly $75 million and thirteen deaths.

Great Boston Fire, 1872.

# Recovering from the Great Boston Fire

Ruins of the burned district.

The spread of flames may have been curtailed by blowing up buildings with gunpowder, leaving gaps that in some cases the fire could not bridge. A controversial tactic at best, this was done at the fervent insistence of the postmaster, William L. Burt, who had help from General Henry Benham, who brought gunpowder from Castle Island, which was where he was posted. The chief fire inspector had reluctantly agreed to try it, and it was not done by approved methods. In the *Report of the Commissioners Appointed to Investigate the Cause and Management of the Great Fire in Boston*, they were castigated for it. The report recommended dynamite in the rare cases when explosives were properly deemed necessary.

Damrell, the chief, received plenty of criticism for the fire, but the facts are in his favor. His modern methods of firefighting later bore out his methods. In fact, *Damrell's Fire*, a **PBS** one-hour documentary on the Great Boston Fire, makes him its hero. In later years, he was recognized by firefighters nationally as a man ahead of his time.

In addition to the physical damage, hundreds of businesses were ruined, many insurance companies went bankrupt from their losses and thousands of citizens of Boston lost their homes, jobs or both.

But the city was still resilient at that time. It was able to recover from the disastrous fire in a surprisingly short amount of time. Firms that were burned out found other quarters, either temporary or permanent ones.

Rebuilding got started almost at once, and within a year the burned-out area had been substantially rebuilt with structures that were of a better quality and that conformed to the new building codes for fire prevention that arose in the aftermath of the conflagration. Pipes, mains and hydrants were replaced, and firefighting equipment was updated by the city, though it was mostly private funds that paid for the rebuilding.

Resilient as Boston proved itself to be, it nonetheless missed an opportunity to renew and improve itself on an even greater scale. The rebuilding could have accomplished that by making wider streets, changing traffic patterns so they would have been easier to maneuver, installing taller buildings and those kinds of things. But the city did not step in and make those things happen.

The first thing that had to be done after the fire was to dispose of the rubble left behind. That was no problem in Boston, which, it seemed, was always looking for material to fill in water or wetlands and make more dry land. In this case, the rubble from the ruined buildings was dumped into Boston Harbor close to shore to fill in what is now Atlantic Avenue.

Many businesses had full insurance—some even more than they needed—so they were able to start rebuilding right away. That meant new buildings that met the stricter building codes. Closed businesses popped up again in strange places as though they were wind-born weeds—on vacant lots, in empty storerooms, in tenement buildings, sometimes a mile away. In the downtrodden Fort Hill area, rows of corrugated iron buildings appeared almost magically to house the boot, shoe and leather trade that later moved to the South Street area near the current South Station.

Although some wanted to widen and straighten the streets, only a small amount of that was done. Those who owned real estate in the area wanted to protect their own holdings and resisted any grand plans for taking property by eminent domain and planning a new business district for which they would have been taxed as abutters. Not only did individuals protect their physical "turf," but municipal agencies also protected their individual authorities, and these often overlapped. So, as a result, nothing got done.

Boston issued bonds to sixteen private property owners in the downtown area so that they would have cash to rebuild. This didn't seem fair to a citizen who lived outside the area, and he sued successfully, arguing that the bonds were a transfer of wealth from one set of citizens to another. So redistribution of wealth was a controversial issue even then.

The things that city planning did accomplish stood in contrast to occasions where it failed. So while Congress and Federal Streets were widened and a new Post Office Square was designed and built, other streets like Summer, Franklin and Devonshire, and Arch and Otis that ran between Summer and Franklin, remained as narrow as ever.

The blasting by the postmaster had saved the partially complete new post office; its solid walls were given credit for stopping the spread of the fire to the north. The new square that bore its name would front on the new post office. The roughly triangular Post Office Square that ran between Congress, Franklin, Milk, Water and Pearl Streets would have other new buildings as well. When Franklin Street was extended past Congress as far north as Broad Street at this time, it became the site of the New England Mutual Life building. A new Equitable Building arose at nearby Milk and Federal Streets—yet another insurance firm.

At mid-century, this had been an area that held banks, warehouses and wholesale and retail businesses, as well as insurance companies. It was convenient to the ocean and to the rail lines and, until that time, held upscale homes such as those of the Perkinses on Pearl Street—homes that later became the Perkins Blind Children's School and Boston Athenaeum. Artist Washington Allston, for whom a section of Brighton is named, had a studio in a barn next to this, which held one of his masterpieces that is now in the Museum of Fine Arts.

But just behind this in the Fort Hill area that rose and descended to the waterfront stood crowded tenements, largely the homes of immigrants who were coming to Boston in ever-greater numbers. The largest group by far was the Irish. By the end of the Civil War, the area was a slum. It burned in the Great Boston Fire, giving way to the buildings that faced the new square. One can suppose that the area would have undergone urban renewal if it had lasted longer.

The slums that were mushrooming around the fine homes of Boston had made many upper- and some middle-class people move to the Back Bay or to outlying areas. Many of the wealthiest moved to Brookline, which was quickly becoming the suburb of choice, enhanced by the addition of public transportation in the form of the train and the trolley. Lack of suitable housing was one factor; the desire to get away from this immigrant enclave was another. Some of those moving to Brookline and other places were those who owned businesses in Boston; others were the professionals and managers who worked for them.

Post Office Square was a bright spot in the rebuilding, and it would have a shining and interesting future. The Federal Reserve Bank opened its first Boston building on the square in 1922 (it later moved to Atlantic Avenue and

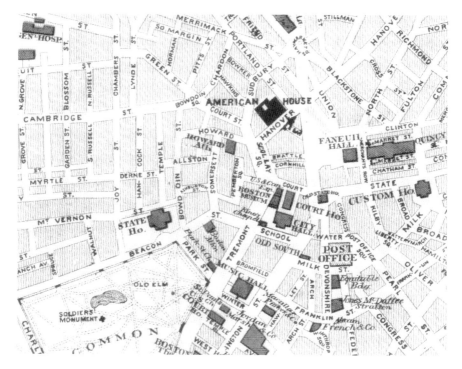

Post Office Square, 1883.

the old building serves now as a hotel). A forty-story office building, One Post Office Square, adjoins it. The square itself saw its first parking garage built there in 1954. The art deco building of the New England Telephone and Telegraph was built on the site of the Perkins houses at Franklin and Pearl Streets in 1947, and the old post office was replaced by the current John W. McCormack Federal Building and Post Office, an impressive art deco building.

The Angell Memorial Fountain was erected as a watering trough in 1912, later surrounded by a small park. A new park, the Norman P. Leventhal Park, was built in the square in 1987 when the Friends of Post Office Square raised over $1 million to demolish the old parking garage and build another underground that reaches eighty feet in depth, the lowest point in the city. The park that followed, a private/public partnership, is perhaps the most popular open space in the city—an urban oasis that is always crowded at lunchtime. It has an all-season restaurant, as well as 125 different kinds of plant life, including trees that provide a canopy of shade for visitors. Those who park in the garage's 1,400 spaces must cross through the park as they enter and leave the garage, providing a steady flow of pedestrians.

# Recovering from the Great Boston Fire

Old Post Office.

Post Office Square and park.

The other square that came to the fore following the Great Boston Fire was Copley Square, named for artist John Singleton Copley. Great institutes of learning and culture arose in that area. Churches from the burned area such as Trinity and New Old South were built so as to anchor diagonal corners of the odd-shaped space, which was first called Art Square.

In the blocks nearby were the first incarnations of M.I.T. (Massachusetts Institute of Technology), Harvard Medical School, the Horace Mann School for the Deaf, Massachusetts College of Art and the Boston Public Library, which was moved from downtown along with the Museum of Fine Arts, both of which faced the square.

The square itself was created after most of the Back Bay was filled in. At that time, Huntington Avenue sliced through the square at an angle that matched its position between the railroad tracks of the Boston & Providence and Boston & Worcester. Its thrust to the southwest was later followed by the Museum of Fine Arts, Symphony Hall, Horticultural Hall, Northeastern University, the New England Conservatory and the Christian Science Church.

Those railroads also had a major impact on Boston. Toward the end of the nineteenth century, five railroads had terminals in Boston—and that was too many. One terminal would do for all the lines that converged in the

Copley Square, 1920.

16

# Recovering from the Great Boston Fire

South Station.

Back Bay and South Cove parts of town, and the one they built was to be the biggest and busiest in the world. Such a terminal was known as a "union station," and the state gave the rights to the Boston Terminal Company, with each of the five lines contributing $100,000. Most of the money, though, was raised by bonds, allowing the company to purchase thirty-five acres along Fort Point Channel near Dewey Square where the station still stands, a location close to downtown and to the docks. It opened on the first day of 1899.

It was an opulent station with many new conveniences, including shops and services inside its high-vaulted great room. Built just in time for the heyday of rail travel, South Station (first called South Central Station) would see 38 million passengers in the year 1913. (To make a comparison, that number of passengers would put an airport in the top twenty busiest in the world in 2010.) In 1945, with servicemen returning from World War II, 135,000 a day went through South Station, a number greater than any railroad station anywhere until then. It declined thereafter, but the building was renovated in the twenty-first century and had its stature restored as a transportation hub.

# Chapter 2

# *Trolleys to Brighton and Brookline Will Go*

The growth of the late nineteenth and early twentieth century called for more transportation, and the next big problem would be to provide it in an orderly way. More people meant more people traveling, and so streetcar lines were built and they spread to all parts of the city and into the suburbs beyond, creating what have been called the "streetcar suburbs." Two of these suburbs were Brighton and Brookline, which, at the time of the Great Boston Fire, were independent towns. But the following year, both reconsidered that independence. Brighton voted in 1873 to become part of Boston and did so in January of the next year. Brookline remained a self-governing town by its own vote in 1873.

Those choices, made by their citizens, would have far-reaching effects. Brookline would shortly thereafter become a wealthy suburb with an easy commute to Boston. Brighton would eventually develop some desirable residential neighborhoods, but unlike Brookline, it would expand its industrial base.

All of this growth, with its burgeoning streetcar lines, especially downtown, meant that the streets became encrusted with vinelike trolley lines. These competing lines sought the same customers, as well as the same space on the streets of the growing towns. However, the trolleys served a purpose, especially the ones that ran out into the suburbs and made it possible for workers to commute into Boston for work. They took tax dollars with them when they moved out of the city but still provided a labor force, mostly skilled workers.

Downtown, the profusion of lines was far worse and so was congestion. It got so bad in the area of the Boston Common that the first subway

Park Street subway station, 1898.

in North America was opened along Tremont Street on September 1, 1897—a splendid engineering feat and an indicator of Boston's forward thinking at that time. But subways and overhead rails didn't stop with that successful dig. Before the end of 1912, tunnels had been built to Cambridge and to East Boston, and elevated trains ran to Roxbury and Charlestown and later to Dorchester.

But it wasn't trains or tunnels but rather trolleys or "street cars" that carried most of the passengers in the late nineteenth and early twentieth centuries. With automobiles still in their infancy, most people were walkers or passengers, and the trolley lines were fighting for their nickels. Suburban towns cheered for the lines that were bringing them new residents, and developers thought all of this transportation and commuting was just great for real estate sales.

Obviously, the competition among the various companies called for some clear-headed person to call for a truce or for some kind of consolidation, and it isn't surprising that this happened only after a small power struggle. The man who spearheaded all of this—and did it cleverly—is little remembered today, but the "star" of this era was Henry M. Whitney, who made remarkable progress and deserves much of the credit for what became the Boston Elevated Railway and later the modern-day "T."

Henry was born and raised near Coolidge Corner in Brookline where Harvard Street crossed a narrow Beacon Street. Beacon Street would be where he would make a small fortune in real estate and transportation. He wanted to make that lane into a modern boulevard with a trolley line, and he began to pick up parcels of real estate along Beacon Street, which, then as now, was one of the principal east–west routes in town, narrow as it was. He didn't spread the word as to what he was doing—kind of like Walt Disney buying up land around Orlando before announcing plans for Disney World. In 1886, Whitney formed a syndicate called the West End Land Company through which he and partner Eugene Knapp then raised $1 million more and bought up more land. He was then able to tell the town that, as a major abutter to Beacon Street, he was willing to donate frontage and thereby pay a major share in the project.

Brookline has always been imbedded within the Boston geographic "frame," but it remained independent. The history of the town from the last part of the nineteenth century into the early twentieth shows how transportation and the growth of the town ran hand in hand and played a major role in determining what kind of town Brookline would turn out to be.

Once known as "Muddy River" when it was a small hamlet on the outskirts of Boston, Brookline was eventually named for the brooks that formed the lines of its northern and southern borders. Hence, "Brookline" was incorporated in 1705. Its first settlement was near today's Brookline Village, where about twenty-five families formed its early nucleus. In the years since then, it grew gradually, spreading out along the routes of transportation that ran through Brookline. Its streets grew like veins and capillaries from these transportation arteries that became the early lifeblood of the town.

One road that appeared in colonial times was the Boston Post Road, which passed through tiny Brookline Village and allowed that to become the retail center of town. That role was reinforced in 1810 when the Boston and Worcester Turnpike ran from Huntington Avenue in Boston and Roxbury, across a bridge over the Muddy River and through the village. That route is today's Route 9 or Boylston Street.

In the nineteenth century, railroads came to town and brought people with them. Most important was the Highland branch of the Boston and Albany, which ran through Brookline Village in 1847 as it passed between Boston and Newton. The other branch of that line—then the Boston and Worcester—paralleled the Charles River and still does, with part of it running through the northern section of Brookline. (It now runs alongside the Massachusetts Turnpike Extension, which crosses under Commonwealth Avenue at the Brighton/Brookline border.) But it was the Highland branch that played a big role in persuading people to move to

# Trolleys to Brighton and Brookline Will Go

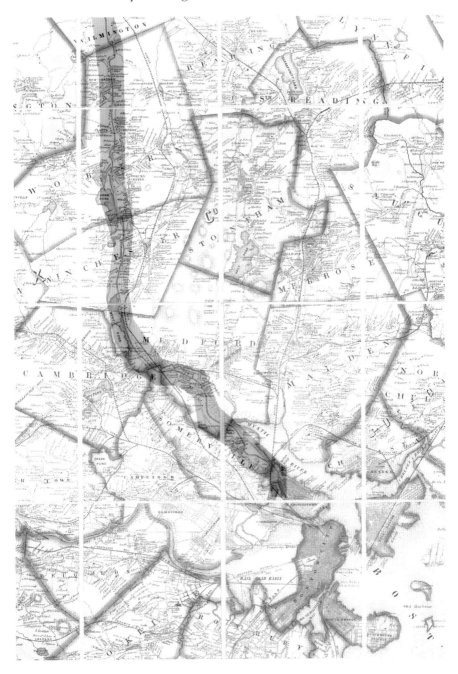

Map of Brookline, 1852 (bottom left area).

Brookline Village.

homes in Brookline and to commute to their work in Boston. Today it is the Riverside line of the T.

Trolleys would have a similar role, particularly along Beacon Street and into the Aberdeen section of Brighton. What would become the Boston Elevated Railway system would run from Kenmore Square to Cleveland Circle as an electrified trolley line, helping Brookline to develop as a streetcar suburb, just as Commonwealth and later Brighton Avenue lines would do for Allston and Brighton.

The section called "Chestnut Hill" developed largely because of the railroad. It brought people—many of them wealthy—to the Chestnut Hill part of Brookline named for the abundance of chestnut trees that grew there. The Chestnut Hill section also covers parts of Newton and Brighton around the reservoir of the same name and at Boston College.

Settlement and commercial development of Chestnut Hill centered at the intersection of Heath and Hammond Streets, near Boylston Street and not far from the new train station. As of 1900, a trolley line also ran along Boylston Street from Newton to Cypress Street, a short distance from Brookline Village.

Streetcar, Green Line.

Boston College and the Chestnut Hill Reservoir.

The streets in the area had large homes of similar styles built on large wooded lots that spoke of gracious living, inviting wealthy Bostonians to move out there. Chestnut Hill, like other neighborhoods of Brookline, appears cohesive because of the similar house types, lots and streets. Though it has variations and urban sections, the town also seems to be of a single piece and more suburban than anything else.

That kind of development was possible elsewhere in Brookline—and in Brighton, too. Henry Whitney was alert to that, but Henry did more than ponder things. Henry was a thinker but also a doer. Traveling into Boston from his home near Coolidge Corner gave him many chances to think of turning Beacon Street into a boulevard that would serve as a thoroughfare for public transportation.

He was thinking of the right thing. Public transportation would be central to growth everywhere, and in Henry's vision, trolleys would run from Kenmore Square to Cleveland Circle, helping Brookline to develop as a streetcar suburb. He would, in time, develop a system that would involve lines on Commonwealth and, later, Brighton Avenue. In fact, Beacon and Commonwealth were closely associated, just as Brookline and Brighton were. The two avenues stretched outward from the Kenmore Square area in lines that were nearly parallel, while Brookline and Brighton lay side by side west of Boston, each developing along their major lines of transportation.

That West End Land Company that Henry Whitney had formed acquired about half of the land it needed to widen Brookline's narrow Beacon Street to two hundred feet when he proposed such a widening to the town's selectmen. The broader picture was this: Henry was also president of the West End Street Railway Company, one of those lines that was vying for passengers in Boston and the suburbs, and he was buying stock in rival companies, too. Henry had two things in mind—bringing trolley service to Beacon Street and developing those parcels of land he had bought on and near Beacon Street. He hired famed landscape architect Frederick Law Olmsted to develop a plan for "the extension of Commonwealth Avenue along Beacon Street."

Beacon Street ran from Beacon Hill where the State House stands, served as an east–west street through Back Bay, crossed Commonwealth Avenue where Kenmore Square is today and ran west from there through Coolidge Corner, Washington Square, Cleveland Circle and on into Newton. It was a means of bringing the northern section of Brookline closer to Brighton and Boston.

When the road was first built, a store and school were put up where Beacon Street crossed Harvard Street, the road to Allston and Roxbury.

The Arcade Building,
Coolidge Corner.

The store (later the site of the S.S. Pierce store) was owned by a man named Coolidge, and the intersection became known as "Coolidge's Corner." It had the town pump and hay scales out front. It would become one of the most-traveled parts of Brookline. A few houses appeared to be sprinkled along Beacon Street, both east and west of Coolidge's Corner, and there were others—some of them quite expensive—on the side of Corey Hill that faced Boston.

About halfway between Coolidge Corner and Cleveland Circle, Beacon Street runs between Corey and Aspinwall Hills at a crossing called Washington Square. For many years before tracks were laid on Beacon Street, these hills had a few farmhouses. It was too far from Boston to become populated. Instead, a passerby would see cows, orchards and woods. The hill on which Timothy Corey had a dairy farm was described in 1800 as "a natural growth of trees and orchards laden with fruit."

Summit Avenue was a new road that ran between Beacon Street and Commonwealth Avenue beginning in 1868 for the benefit of the farms on Corey Hill, but its route—right up over the summit of the hill—provided a magnificent panorama from the 260-foot summit that included a splendid view of Boston. It became such a popular viewing point that the town built a walkway and later stairs to the summit from Washington Square at Beacon and Washington Streets where large estates were being built, including one called Stonehurst for Eben Jordan of Boston's Jordan Marsh department store, remnants of which still remain.

In 1900, the town bought parcels of land at the summit for a park. This was a good thing because Whitney's trolley would bring increasing demand and development to the terraced roads along the hillside, and this forward thinking stymied the impulse for overdevelopment that would come in the decades ahead.

Henry Whitney's plans called for a horsecar trolley or cable car line to run along Beacon Street. Whitney, who was also a Brookline park commissioner, knew Frederick Law Olmsted from his work on the Riverway between Brookline Village and Jamaica Plain and wanted to tap him to design the area, calling him "a man who stands second to none in this land for laying out avenues of this kinds, whose fame extends from Maine to Mexico."

Olmsted may have had no rival, but Whitney did. A rival railway company opposed the plan because it wanted to lay the tracks itself. It controlled the small section at the Boston end of the line where the Beacon Street lane ran, and it was dragging its feet on agreement. Whitney wouldn't put up with this. "There's only one way to get rid of these railways," he said. "We'll have to buy them all." And he did.

He had been planning for this day, and he rode right over his opponents by acquiring all the major horse-car companies in Boston and making them part of his syndicate. He then went ahead, offering a grandiose plan that would turn Beacon Street into a lordly boulevard. His plan called for a two-hundred-foot avenue with two bridle paths, a commercial lane, a pleasure drive, one lane for walking or bicycling and streetcar tracks. All of these were to be separated by rows of trees—no surprise, considering Olmsted's involvement. So it would be a leafy boulevard, and much of it remains so.

Alas! It was too grandiose and too expensive. Even with Whitney contributing $150,000 of his own, he had to reduce the width to a piddling 160 feet and forget about the bridle and cycling paths before the selectmen would approve it. Whitney wasn't badly bashed, though.

Of course real estate sold briskly along this new boulevard with all its amenities and also the promise that three thousand elm and maple trees would be added. Single-family homes were the first to be built, but they weren't financially viable since the land was so valuable and prices so high. So row houses replaced them, as did apartment blocks and stores.

Olmsted's plan for the area was to develop it residentially around the trolley line. (Today such a plan would be called "smart growth.") A substantial residential area would arise between Beacon Street and Commonwealth Avenue, most but not all of it in Brookline.

After they cross one another near Kenmore Square, Beacon Street and Commonwealth Avenue run roughly parallel and often rather close together. That's especially true from Washington Square through Cleveland Circle's

Aberdeen section with its many Scottish street names, and Whitney bought some parcels of land that were actually in Brighton (though near Beacon Street), so his trolley lines helped to people a wide swath of land.

As we know, Olmsted based Commonwealth Avenue in the Back Bay on the four-hundred-foot-wide boulevards like those in Paris that were familiar to him. After its grandly formed Back Bay portion of the street, Commonwealth Avenue ran parallel to the Charles River and then wound west to the Chestnut Hill Reservoir, where it connected to Beacon Street by part of Chestnut Hill Avenue, roads known as the "Chestnut Hill Loop." An original Olmsted plan shows the part of Commonwealth west of Warren Street as a meandering roadway bordered by trees in an Olmsted-like manner. Thus, Olmsted/Whitney were producing a new urban/suburban phenomenon—the parkway/boulevard that linked the city with its suburbs.

Brighton's Commonwealth Avenue and Brookline's Beacon Street were projected at about the same time, both based on Olmsted plans, and a lively competition arose between them for investment and development. However, the city of Boston did not develop the Brighton part of Commonwealth Avenue as quickly as a competition would suggest, and the streetcar lines along that boulevard were not finished until 1909, by which time Beacon Street was already thriving. Real estate values in Brookline remained higher as years went by, validating its decision to become independent of Boston.

The other major change Whitney made to public transit was in replacing his notion of horsecars and cable cars with a better idea. Whitney came to see that electric trolley cars like those being run in Richmond, Virginia, by Henry Sprague were the coming thing. Whitney had seen them and watched tests whose success erased his doubts. He realized that electric lines were the future of public transportation, so he ordered the cars and ordered the tracks for them to run on at the end of September 1887. It was one of those business gambles that thrust some companies and some technologies ahead of those run by people who are too cautious to make a bold move. Even then, some people told Whitney that he was crazy; others said he would wind up electrocuting them, but he went ahead.

The tracks Whitney ordered would form a public transit line that would run through Coolidge Corner to Cleveland Circle—with electrification—beginning on January 1, 1889. Whitney's system became the model for other systems around the country.

It would be a system, not just one line. In fact, West End's first electric trolley line was built between Union Square Allston and Park Square in the

Washington Square, Beacon Street.

Back Bay. (Those who like local trivia may want to know that Boston's first bus route also ran from Union Square in 1922 to Faneuil Square in Brighton.)

Boston's use of electric traction for its large rapid transit system was a first, but it didn't happen without more problem solving. The main problem was to acquire sufficient electric power. These lines were being built in a day when there were no electric grids and no way to provide the needed power at a reasonable price. (Streetcar lines wanted to charge only five cents so that they could attract more riders and eventually populate more suburban areas.) Whitney's system also had color-coded routes and signs showing the destination of vehicles as part of the first electrified and largest streetcar system in the world.

Public power was not sufficient and much of it was direct current (DC), which could not be transmitted great distances from Boston anyway. So, in order to power its electric lines, the railway company had to build its own power stations, placing them in Boston, Allston, Cambridge, Dorchester, Charlestown, East Cambridge and East Boston. Within a few years, these power plants were capable of generating thirty-six megawatts. The system

Central power station.

had over four hundred miles of tracks for its 1,550 streetcars and sixteen miles of elevated track with 174 trains.

Then, in 1911, a huge generator of alternating current (AC) was built in South Boston. Electricity from this generator could be transmitted many miles at high voltage to substations that would then drop the level of the voltage so it could be used on the system. When completed in 1931, this system would have fourteen substations. This was a system that the Boston Elevated Railway and then the T used for many years. It wasn't until 1981 that the system switched to public utilities for its power. So within a few years, Whitney and Olmsted and those who came after them had given Boston an excellent public transit system that would become the Boston Elevated Railway and then the MBTA or "T." These men would also give us the leafy Beacon Street, still one of the finest boulevards in the area.

Brighton, in 1874, had become part of Boston, as we'll discuss in more detail later. Brookline had spurned the opportunity. When these things happened, the borders between them were slightly altered in order to open a "corridor" between the eastern part of Brighton called "Allston" and Back Bay at Kenmore Square. That allowed the separate parts of Boston to be contiguous with one another. However, this new corridor cut Brookline off from the shore of the Charles River.

The northern border of Brookline ran roughly between the later Commonwealth Avenue and Beacon Street. This redrawing also put both Kenmore Square and Packard's Corner (where Commonwealth Avenue and Brighton Avenue meet) slightly outside the Brookline border.

Even at this time, Brighton was more industrial than Brookline and had financial difficulties, too. But in this context, it was largely the Beacon Street–Commonwealth Avenue competition that separated Brighton and Brookline both in terms of development and wealth. Olmsted (who by now lived in Brookline) had rolled out his concept for Commonwealth Avenue in 1885, and the road itself was built in stages over the next decade. But it took Boston far longer to get it done than Brookline had with Beacon Street.

Beacon Street, also an Olmsted design, involved the widening of a street that was already there and making it a green boulevard in keeping with Whitney's concept. Along with the widening came the tracks, and along those tracks came the trolley, so development continued apace. This was not true in Allston or Brighton, where its sister boulevard was built in stages and with no tracks or trolleys to help it develop at first.

The trackless and largely undeveloped Commonwealth was nonetheless ballyhooed as it was completed. Its first few miles from Kenmore Square to Packard's Corner in Allston were followed by a swing to the left, and then several wide curves bringing it at last to Chestnut Hill. It was called "the prime driveway of our city."

A driveway, of course, implied houses, and these would not appear soon in any number. Yet it was fit for a president if not for a king; our twenty-third president, Benjamin Harrison, used it, as reported in the *Brighton Item* in August 1888: "It is no wonder that Bostonians are proud of the avenue, or that [President Benjamin Harrison] on Wednesday last should have been driven over it as Boston's most finished, and it might be added polished, driveway."

The path of the road wound through areas of fields and ledges and rocky outcrops, but it was an area with fewer than ten buildings. That made it easier to get the land, and much of it was donated to the tune of about $425,000. The men—mostly real estate holders—who donated land compared Commonwealth with Beacon Street, noting that Beacon would cost more to build because Whitney didn't own enough of the land and Corey's Hill was in the way. They also dismissed wealthy Brookline, which would not spend taxpayers' money on it. They urged Boston to hasten completion of Commonwealth Avenue, at taxpayer expense.

# Trolleys to Brighton and Brookline Will Go

For about half a million dollars, the city did this by the close of 1888 as far as Chestnut Hill Reservoir. It, too, was two hundred feet wide with a single roadway of stone covered in tar and gravel pedestrian paths on the sides.

Again, the *Brighton Item* took pride in the new road:

> [From] *the junction of Brighton Avenue...* [it] *winds to the left, and here we have a magnificent roadway, as smooth as a floor, though of course, not as level, but nicely rounding from the center to the gutters* [to facilitate drainage]. *As the grade rises above Allston Street there appears to have been some washing of the successive hillsides up to beyond Warren Street, but these have been properly repaired, and the excellent general character of the roadway maintained.*
>
> *After the second hill is surmounted the settled way of unsurpassed excellence is again met with; but on the rise above Washington Street there is a slight washing on the surface and the sides of the avenue, but this would be hardly noticed on any other but this almost perfect macadam way. As the avenue inclines downward on the western slope of the hill, there are also to be seen slight indications of washing of the surface, and then beyond the Chestnut Hill Reservoir entrance the way* [the Chestnut Hill Reservoir Driveway] *is in splendid condition.*

Beacon Street, on the other hand, had town improvements like sewers and utilities and advantages like side streets with house lots and even some houses. Most importantly, it had those trolleys, and they would not mount the towering hills of Commonwealth Avenue on a completed circuit until 1909, twenty-one years after the road was built. Even though the city of Boston increased its assessments, and thus its taxes, on the presumed value of the avenue, development was painfully slow and those values were nonexistent.

Now the *Item*'s verbiage turned sour: "Commonwealth Avenue has been built at an expense of nearly half a million dollars, and there is not yet a house upon it from old Brighton Avenue [Packard Corner] to the Chestnut Hill Reservoir."

Whitney had a lot to do with Beacon Street's easy win in this financial and transportation competition between a private entity and a municipality. But while both streets would eventually command high real estate prices, Beacon Street would always hold the advantage of being closer to downtown and located in a more prestigious milieu. Brookline, which had eschewed the advantages of joining Boston, could take deserved pride in its well-kept parks and streets, fine schools and other excellent public services. It was even the birthplace of John F. Kennedy.

Still, the Brighton businessmen didn't go easily into the night. In 1891, sixty-five of them petitioned the city to get it going: "We believe the completion…will prove a great and permanent benefit to the city, because it will create new and desirable investments, and will retain here capital (that is) now being diverted to Beacon Street in Brookline."

The city did get going on the next phase of the development, and the Brighton people liked what they saw. The avenue had 20-foot setbacks on each side, which meant it was 240 feet wide from building to building, making it wider than Beacon Street. It also had sidewalks from Packard's Corner to Warren Street, carriage roads and grassy plots on each side, as well as trees.

Also, the developers did not foresee the rise of apartment buildings along the avenue. They pictured the building of large-scale, high-style detached houses—the sort of development that was occurring in the Aberdeen Section near the Reservoir, along Englewood, Strathmore and Sutherland, as well as Commonwealth. Much of this was due to the earlier development of Beacon Street up to Cleveland Circle. Developers expected a higher class of people to live in the areas along Commonwealth Avenue.

In part, a declining economy hurt them. The depression of 1893, like many such downturns, destroyed the real estate market. By 1899, only four buildings stood on Commonwealth Avenue, and promised improvements had not been made, even though the depression was over. Beacon Street was the place to live. It already had those electric streetcars, while Commonwealth had none and wouldn't for another decade.

Even in 1909, however, only six buildings stood between Packard's Corner and Warren Street, and there were no houses at all between Warren Street and Wallingford Road, about two miles farther west. On the upper reaches of the boulevard near the Aberdeen neighborhood that was developing, seven homes had been built, and there were none beyond the reservoir.

All of those areas would be built upon in the years to come, and Allston-Brighton would become a desirable residential location. Commonwealth Avenue, by then, was a wide, well-traveled and, indeed, handsome boulevard. Brighton could, after all, be green and leafy like Brookline—at least part of it could.

# Chapter 3

# *Brookline, Brighton and the Parting of Ways*

Brookline was on its way to differentiating itself from Brighton and other communities. "Greenness" had been a feature Brookline had strived for and would continue to work for even as it became more urban. In fact, the famed landscape gardener Andrew Jackson Downing had this to say about a newly built part of town called the Lindens near St. Mary's of the Assumption Church and not far from Brookline Village:

> *The whole of this neighborhood of Brookline is a kind of landscape garden, and there is nothing in America of the sort, so inexpressibly charming as the lanes which lead from one cottage, or villa, to another…tempting vistas and glimpses under the pendent boughs, give it quite an Arcadian air of rural freedom and enjoyment. These lanes are clothed with a profusion of trees and wild shrubbery, often almost to the carriage tracks, and curve and wind about, in a manner quite bewildering to the stranger who attempts to thread them alone; and there are more hints here for the lover of the picturesque in lanes than we ever saw assembled together in so small a compass.*

Downing used the vocabulary of his time, which was more flowery than the sparse prose of our time. But the look of Brookline has been remarkably preserved, at least in its nonurban areas. We might say "leafy" rather than "picturesque" and "quiet" instead of "Arcadian," and the town has seen considerable development since that was written, but it still maintains a considerable amount of green space in many of its neighborhoods.

Linden Square, Brookline.

Longwood, of course, is one of them—at least in part. The five hundred acres of Longwood and the Cottage Farm areas that were bought by David Sears provide examples. The Riverway, which ran through Longwood, early on became a part of the Emerald Necklace of Olmsted. Sears also hired a well-known civil engineer, Alexander Wadsworth, who was a designer of Mount Auburn Cemetery, to lay out his huge estate so that it would have residential neighborhoods with parks and squares and thousands of trees—whose species he specified. That proved to be one way to preserve a leafy area within an urban setting—buy it and set it out so that it becomes difficult to change. It only takes money and thought.

A part of Brookline that would evolve quite differently is the Harvard Street area, which became a mixed residential and commercial area with some historic sites as well. Harvard Street runs from Brookline Village to Allston, where it becomes Harvard Avenue. Beals Street, about halfway between Coolidge Corner and the Allston border, can boast the birthplace of John F. Kennedy. The house, owned then by Joseph and Rose Kennedy, still stands on this quiet, leafy street. The church and school JFK attended, St. Aiden's, is a short distance away. Today it is no longer a church but mixed-income housing. Nonetheless, it is on the National Register of Historic Places.

Not far from the historic Kennedy birthplace on Beals Street is the 1740 Edward Devotion House on Harvard Street, and the school named for him stands behind it, originally built from his donation. The school is the most recent of several that have stood here. This house is located on busy Harvard Street, which still has apartment houses but also a good deal of commercial development. These areas were part of a major residential development that followed the trolley's installation on Beacon Street.

# Brookline, Brighton and the Parting of Ways

Edward Devotion House, Harvard Street, Brookline.

The major shopping area that includes Coolidge Corner is nearby. In time, Coolidge Corner overtook Brookline Village as the commercial center of town. It still has interesting and historical buildings from the early 1900s like the Arcade Building, a two-story building that has shops and offices within an atrium; the Coolidge Theatre, known for its showing of classic and genre films; and the S.S. Pierce Building, now a pharmacy. Diagonally across Beacon Street from this stands the modernist Patriot Bank/Brookline Trust Company building from 1912. The area has a significant Jewish population and a temple, Kehillath Israel, on the south side of Harvard Street. The remainder of Harvard Street between Coolidge Corner and Brookline Village contains apartments, churches and commercial buildings, with the latter becoming more frequent as you near its juncture with Washington Street, near Brookline Village.

In South Brookline, the town also can boast of the 1882 Country Club, site of many sports events and of local golfer Francis Ouimet's upset victory in the 1913 U.S. Open. There is also Larz Anderson Park, sixty-four acres donated by the family of the former diplomat who owned the estate. It contains the Putterham School, a one-room colonial schoolhouse, and an antique auto museum within a carriage house. Part of it is in Jamaica Plain, near Olmsted's Emerald Necklace, and the Boston skyline can be seen from its highest point.

Olmsted chose Brookline, too, and he chose one of the leafier parts of town. In 1883, he bought the Clark house on Warren Street for both his home and office. Brookline was, after all, where his friend H.H. Richardson, architect of Trinity Church, and many others lived. Richardson's home was

Harvard and Washington Streets.

Larz Anderson estate.

just a short walk distant on Cottage Street, and another neighbor was Charles Sprague Sargent, the director of Arnold Arboretum, also an Olmsted design.

Olmsted played a central role in the Brighton/Brookline part of this story, as well as in the preservation of Boston's green space. He had also designed Ringer's Playground in Allston-Brighton, with its hilly wooded and rocky areas along with playing fields and tennis courts, a combination that set it apart from the average urban park. His Brookline/Jamaica Plain sections of the "Emerald Necklace," not far from his new home, make this seem like a fitting location for what would become in 1979 the Frederick Law Olmsted National Historic Site.

Apart from Olmsted, members of Boston's Brahmin class also bought estates in Brookline. Perhaps most notable was Thomas Handasyd Perkins, the "Merchant Prince" of the China trade. His museumlike estate was on Cottage Street, as were those of Samuel Cabot and William Gardiner. Perkins, an international trader, brought in rare species of plants from around the world and grew them on his estate.

This type of country estate was far more common in Brookline than in Brighton, which had only a few. The two towns, with their many similarities

Olmsted National Historic Site.

of geography and location, became two different places. This was implicit to some extent in their early history, but it became more obvious once the questions of annexation by Boston were settled in each town.

Boston had "won" five in a row of these annexation votes before Brookline broke that streak. That had widespread ramifications, too, as other wealthy towns across America also declined annexation by a nearby core city.

Though Brookline shared a border with Brighton on its north and the towns had some similarities of geography and terrain, they diverged sharply, too, especially after 1873 when the question of annexation was decided. Brookline kept its independence, thus making its own rules and raising taxes on its citizens when necessary to pay for its services, which were top notch.

One exception was the water supply. At the time it declined annexation, Brookline's water came from the Charles River six miles away (actually from wells on the banks of that river). The water was pumped through conduits to the top of Fisher's Hill, where there was a reservoir.

Brighton shared Boston's better water supply from Lake Cochichuate, using storage basins at the Chestnut Hill Reservoir, which had the right elevation

Brookline Reservoir, Boylston Street.

to allow the water flow. In 1902, Brookline bought Boston's old reservoir off Route 9 between Lee and Warren Streets to use for its water supply.

We've seen that Brookline was cut off from the Charles River so that Brighton, then a part of Boston, could be joined with the rest of the city. One other geographic oddity was that the annexation and nonannexation now separated Brookline, in Norfolk County, from the rest of the county since West Roxbury, which bordered Brookline on the southwest, became part of Boston in 1874; this made it, like Brighton, a part of Suffolk County. The nearest town to Brookline that was in the same county was Dedham. A quick glance at a map of the metropolitan area gives the appearance that Brookline was "scooped out" of Boston. Actually, Brighton, West Roxbury, Roxbury and Hyde Park became part of Boston. Only Brookline did not.

Many of the new residents of Brookline commuted daily to Boston from businesses they owned or to jobs in those companies. Brookline was now convenient due to the railroad and trolley lines, and it offered an "escape" from a city that, to their minds, was becoming overrun with immigrants. Population growth was steady, mostly with upper-class people moving from Boston.

The rural nature of the town that had remained during the earlier infusion of residents changed in the later decades of the nineteenth century, however, as farmers received offers for their lands that they could not refuse. These people lived on the land they worked, and it didn't matter that this land was farther from Boston since they only had to go there to sell their products—and that was an occasional thing. So farms were subdivided and became estates for the wealthy and the well-to-do. These were often businessmen or professionals.

For all of that, Brookline could look forward to a lot of building—roads and parks and homes and apartment buildings. And these people that the town was attracting were not the sort who could or would do that kind of work. They were not day laborers. As in most of these situations, the obvious answer to this one was the immigrant Irish, so many of whom had crowded into Boston. At first Brookline had very few Irish, but that would change.

Irish moved in near the Muddy River in a section with three-deckers and inexpensive housing called "The Marsh" on the eastern side of town between the railroad tracks and Brookline Avenue. They also settled on the west side of the village in an area known as "Whisky Point" (or later "The Point"). Both areas had light industry nearby. In truth, though it was close to Brookline Village, it was still a ghetto. The Irish population in Brookline grew steadily, reaching 40 percent by the end of the nineteenth century.

Though confined to their "own" area, as they were in Boston, the Brookline Irish were better off in terms of chances for upward mobility. Men worked mostly as day laborers, women as domestics. Brookline had plenty of good-paying work for them, even a chance to start small businesses in the trades, and those who lived in town had first pick when work became available because they were already in town and some of them were establishing reputations for reliability and workmanship. By the turn of the century, there was an Irish middle class, even a few upper-class people like Thomas B. Fitzpatrick. Fitzpatrick had worked for a firm in Boston that had been driven out of business by the Great Boston Fire of 1872. He then became a partner and later sole partner in a dry goods business. He owned a fine estate on Winthrop Road.

The elite in town learned to live with the Irish, but not without distaste. They worried about the poor housing conditions and crowdedness in a marshy area that was likely to bring disease. These Irish were Catholics whereas most of the upper class were Protestants; this was a source of friction, too. But in the end, Brookline had essentially two groups: the wealthy, most of whom worked or did business in Boston, and the lower-class Irish who did the work that needed to be done in town. Most of the voters liked the way the town was headed, and it wasn't hard to decide against annexation by better than four to one.

Brookline was able to withstand joining the parade, unlike Brighton and West Roxbury in the same year, Dorchester three years earlier in a contentious vote and Roxbury two years before that. All of these increased Boston's area and the number of its people. Some of these towns were won over by the promise of city services like sewer systems and an excellent water supply.

By then, however, Brookline had taught itself that it was more capable of running things than the larger city would be. Many also liked the idea of making decisions that would shape the town in the way they wanted. Brookline eventually had a town meeting kind of government, which allowed all the male voters to participate in debating every measure and voting on each, while a five-member board of selectmen served as the executives. Boston, during this time, had a mayor and two representative bodies who governed for them.

The Irish favored annexation as well since it protected the kind of "closed shop" they had. If the town became part of the larger city, the pool of workers would be larger and their chances for good jobs less likely. Separation was good; they wished to keep it.

# Brookline, Brighton and the Parting of Ways

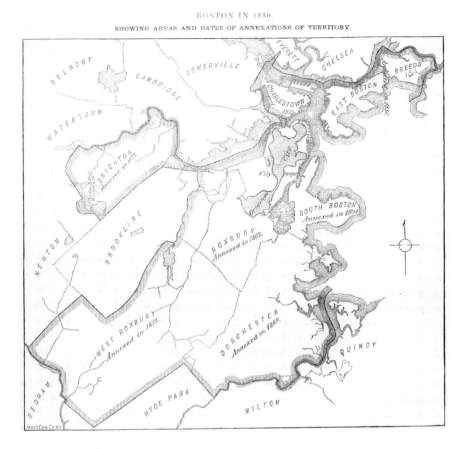

Annexations by Boston.

Brighton favored annexation. A lot of the reason for that choice can be traced back to its history.

Location is important in deciding whether a particular town or city will have an important role to play in history. Brighton had a favorable location in nineteenth-century history. It was the gateway from the west to Boston. Brighton was located on the Charles River, which would later have a dam at the Boston end, and was on a mainline of the Boston and Worcester Railroad. It also had roads that ran through it from Watertown and Cambridge to Brookline and Roxbury and into Boston. So Brighton had the things needed to become a transportation center—and it did.

Its town fathers exploited that location as good entrepreneurs have always done. The industries that gathered there during that period suited its location and took advantage of its assets.

Brighton Center.

The eastern section, later called Allston, had good soil for farming and was close to Boston, where its products could be marketed. Access was even easier after the Mill-Pond road was built across the Charles River from near Kenmore Square.

In addition to the Commonwealth Avenue area in Allston and Brighton that would become developed in the early 1900s, the section around Brighton Center and North Brighton also developed. In the 1840s, Brighton became an important gardening center and still is.

More memorable, perhaps, was the establishment of the Cattle Fair Hotel in Brighton Center, around which the cattle marketing trade grew up. This industry was later moved down Market Street to North Brighton, where a large slaughterhouse was built near the banks of the Charles along the Boston and Worcester Railroad line. This was not completely a positive thing for a residential area, since the unpleasant odor from the facility would be carried for miles on a windy day.

Allied to farming was market gardening, which was a small-scale operation where many type of vegetables and fruits were grown for direct sale at roadside stands or to nearby markets, restaurants or stores. These farms were labor intensive, using farmhands rather than plows or other mechanized devices. Some fruits and vegetables were grown in greenhouses. These low-volume sales were made during the growing season, which meant that the owners needed some other sideline for the cold weather months.

Greenhouses could also grow flowers during many seasons because their glass panes trapped the solar radiation, allowing the plants to absorb them. Brighton also became a horticultural center during the mid-nineteenth century, one of the leading ones in the Boston area. Several companies are still in business today. Perhaps the best known was Joseph Breck's near Oak Square. The seed catalogues are still used today, but at that time, Breck was editor of the *New England Farmer* and author of *The Young Florist*.

Brighton also had the Winships, especially Jonathan, who founded Winship's Gardens, and William C. Strong, whose vineyard in the western part of town near the Newton line was one of the largest in the country. He also contributed writing to the craft of agriculture, his best-known work being *Cultivation of the Grape*.

Despite this agrarian prominence, Brighton will perhaps best be remembered for its role in the cattle trade. During the American Revolution, Jonathan Winthrop I and II made "Little Cambridge," as Brighton was known at that time, into a collection point for cattle to be used in the war effort. Washington's headquarters was located at the Cragie House near Harvard, and much of the besieging American army was gathered at Harvard.

Brighton continued in that role after the war, even after separating from Cambridge and becoming an independent town in 1807. By that time, the cattle and slaughtering business was dominant, and it was Cambridge's failure to make improvements considered important to the transportation of this industry that led to the divorce. Cambridge failed to replace the bridge between the Harvard area and Little Cambridge, so the residents of that area formed their own town and called it Brighton.

This trade coalesced around events collectively called the Brighton Cattle Market, located in the hilly area south of Brighton Center, which later held civic and educational buildings. It was called Agricultural Hill. At the bottom of it, not far west of Brighton Center along Washington Street, was the huge Cattle Fair Hotel, boasting one hundred rooms as the largest hotel in the area outside of Boston. Its manager, Zachariah Porter, knew how to cater to upper-class patrons. Porter later founded the Porter House Hotel in Cambridge whose name is today also associated with beef in porterhouse steak. In all, Brighton had fifteen hotels. Many of these bragged about their excellent bars, but the rowdy behavior of the bars' patrons provided another reason for potential residents to resist Brighton.

The stockyards lay behind the large hotel, and on market day, all of Brighton Center swarmed with the dealers who stayed at the hotel along with their bevies of bovines, especially in October when the Brighton Fair and Cattle Show was held. By the time of the Civil War, Brighton had over forty slaughterhouses and many factories that made byproducts such as tallow and fertilizer. The town's manufacturing output was rivaled only by Boston.

All of this financial success had a negative side. It was becoming obvious, for example, that the location of the cattle industry at the center of town was no longer a good idea. On the face of it, that kind of thing had to be away from residential areas and near lines of transportation like roads, railroads and rivers. People, especially the well-to-do, weren't moving to Brighton so that they could live near the livestock trade. In fact, population growth was slow. Not only that, but even in this era before Upton Sinclair's *The Jungle*, concerns had been raised about how safe and how clean our food was, especially in Massachusetts.

Brighton Center, on the other hand, was valuable real estate for other things like houses and stores. The industrial things belonged somewhere more isolated. North Brighton was such an area. It already had small industries, and the railroad ran through there as did the post road, and the river was nearby. It also had open land that could be used. It made sense to

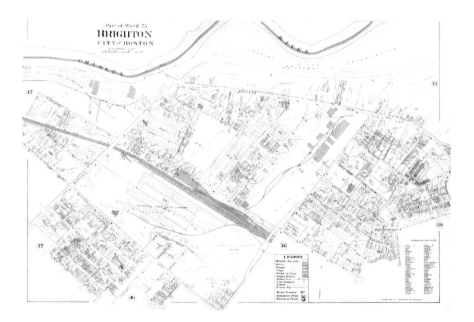

Map showing the stockyards.

centralize the industry, to raise standards and allow inspections before these were forced down the throat of the town. Besides, the meat industry as a suburban profit center was bound to come to an end with changes to the meatpacking industry, and Brighton would need to look in other directions through which to sustain.

A group of town leaders led by state senator William Warren got together to move the livestock industry and improve the amenities of the town. That was a large bite to take, and like many ambitious people who like to see results, they tried to do too much in a short time. The stockyards were placed in North Brighton on the west side of Market Street, and an abattoir was built there, too.

But the Warren group also saw to it that infrastructure was built—roads, sewerage, utilities, parks, civic buildings and the like. These things were needed. They had been neglected to this point. Brighton, at this time, also had fine public buildings, excellent firefighting equipment and good schools.

But rather than raise taxes and thereby discourage potential residents, they used deficit spending—four dollars for every dollar of revenue. They borrowed the rest at high rates of interest, and in only four years, Brighton's debt became eight times worse than it had been.

If you've read about or lived through other eras of history where this was done, you know that it doesn't work well. Brighton paid the piper by giving up its independence. Having run the town into a dead end of

Brighton Library.

debt, the Warren cabal (who also made a tidy sum of its own by selling real estate to the town at inflated prices) had a no-pain solution to all the red ink—they would let Boston pay for it after the city had annexed them. After all, Boston had plenty of money just then. They were able to convince their fellow townsmen, who voted four to one to become a part of Boston; on January 1, 1874, it did.

To some extent, Brighton did become suburban in nature, at least the areas that had easy access to public transportation. The section nearest to Boston was such a case. It was called "Allston" after the painter Washington Allston who had lived just across the river. It is the only town in the country named for a painter. It was also the closest to Boston, across the milldam, and it contained the road to Cambridge.

After the Civil War, the railroad—now called the Boston & Albany—was making buckets of money from the cattle trade, and in the last decades of the nineteenth century, it built or upgraded its facilities with rail yards in Allston that would later become the location of the Massachusetts Turnpike extension. They built repair shops, a classification yard, two roundhouses and loading facilities, becoming the largest taxpayer in Allston-Brighton.

The community already had people who commuted to Boston. From 1858 on, this travel was by horse-drawn trolleys that ran through Oak Square, Brighton Center and Union Square. However, the railroad offered improved services for passengers from the 1880s on, including stone depots designed by the famed architect Henry Hobson Richardson at Faneuil Street, Brighton (Market Street) and Allston. The Allston depot alone survives, serving now as a restaurant.

Electric streetcars made the largest contribution to development. A trolley housed in a car barn on Allston's Braintree Street made the first trip on this electrified device. The lines on Commonwealth Avenue and Brighton Avenue would come later.

"Brighton Avenue" was the name given to the road between Packard's Corner where Commonwealth Avenue curved to the left and Union Square, Allston. From that junction, the street crossing through the square from southwest to northeast was Cambridge Street. It ran from Cambridge to Brighton Center. North Beacon Street ran to the northwest off Union Square and crossed the bridge over the Charles River into Watertown.

After Commonwealth Avenue left Kenmore Square, it ran to Packard's Corner where it met Brighton Avenue. From Packard's Corner, Commonwealth Avenue winds west. Rows of apartment building blocks built at that time may still be seen along the route of the trolley.

Packard's Corner.

## ALVAN FULLER AND THE AUTO MILE

Packard's Corner was named for a successful livery stable and riding school established there by John D. Packard and his sons. The area began to grow following the trolley line that was built in 1909. The part of Commonwealth Avenue that ran from there east toward Kenmore Square eventually became known as the "Auto Mile," beginning with Alvan T. Fuller's establishment of a car dealership at the corner named for the horseman.

Fuller, an extremely clever businessman, opened a Packard automobile dealership at the intersection that already bore that name. It seemed a good fit. Fuller was also a successful politician and, in 1924, defeated James M. Curley in the race for governor of Massachusetts.

Just as the railroad and the trolley car would play major roles in the growth of our communities during the nineteenth century, that role in the twentieth century would belong to the automobile, and an area of Allston-Brighton/Brookline would be its home on behalf of Boston during that time. Its influence would be both positive and negative, and its focal point

Alvan T. Fuller.

would be along Commonwealth and Brighton Avenues, roughly from Cottage Farm (later B.U.) Bridge west to Union Square Allston and North Beacon Street Brighton, with its center point at Packard's Corner.

In another sense, it would center on a single person, Alvan T. Fuller, who was both a brilliant businessman and a successful politician. Since Fuller, in many ways, exemplified the best of this period, he is worth looking at. Born in Charlestown, he moved to Malden at an early age and at sixteen began to work in a rubber factory. At night he repaired and sold bicycles, and to call attention to his business, he began to race them, becoming a champion by winning most of his races with a slow start and dynamic finish—a metaphor that fit most of his later political life. Soon afterward, he moved to Columbia Road in Boston.

Though bicycles were fine and fun and a financial plus, Fuller could see that automobiles were the vehicles of the future. He sold his racing trophies to pay for his voyage to Europe, where he learned more about the auto industry that had taken hold there. He managed to buy two cars and bring them back—the first cars to be imported into Boston.

Next he talked the Packard Motor Company of Detroit into giving him the Boston area's exclusive dealership. He added a Cadillac agency as well, sharing a building with other dealers before moving in 1908 to the happily named Parckard's Corner. There he built his automobile emporium, not far from where Edward Packard's livery service had been.

His building was a departure from the usual fume-filled garage where cars were sold. It was a huge building with a first-floor showroom that most resembled the lobby of a fancy hotel—except that it had new cars on the floor as well as chairs and sofas. The floors above were used for putting the cars together and equipping them, for repair bays and the storage of parts and accessories.

Packard's Corner was practically empty when Fuller moved there—but it didn't stay that way for long. Other auto dealers followed, and by the end of the First World War, at least a dozen existed along Commonwealth and

Brookline, Brighton and the Parting of Ways

Brighton Avenues as the beginning of Boston's Auto Mile. Then it really took off. Besides dealers, all kinds of automobile-related businesses sprang up during the '20s on these streets, as well as on North Beacon Street off Union Square.

You could get tires, springs, batteries, speedometers, chrome accessories, radiators—anything having to do with cars in over one hundred locations. There were also trucks and used cars, of course.

Alvan Fuller did much to promote Allston and Brighton as an automobile center. He is probably best known for having started the Washington's Birthday open houses. Other dealers followed suit, so by the 1920s, you could walk up or down Commonwealth Avenue visiting showrooms, enjoying promotions and picking out your next car. It was Fuller, too, who brought about trade-ins and time payments. The advent of automobile use during this time also marked a temporary end to most expansion of the public transportation system, although that would resume later in the century.

At about that time, Fuller erected a building for his Cadillac dealership at 808 Commonwealth Avenue, a beautiful building now part of Boston University that can be seen today from the Massachusetts Turnpike, which runs beneath it on that extension. But once he had become the world's leading dealer, Fuller moved more solidly into politics, beginning an interesting career that ended on a note of irony.

Fuller had already entered politics at that point, winning seats in the state legislature by razor-thin margins and then doing the same in a race for Congress. In 1920, he became lieutenant governor and then defeated James Michael Curley, twice mayor of Boston, to become governor of Massachusetts. He served ably and was reelected, remaining popular until the trial of Sacco and Vanzetti, immigrant radicals who were sentenced to death after they were convicted of killing two men during an armed robbery in Braintree.

Sacco and Vanzetti were believed to belong to radical groups at a time when America was going through a "Red Scare." Their affiliations may have caused their demise as much as the crimes they were charged with.

The trial had irregularities, and the verdict may have been at least partially wrong. Supporters of the two men, especially immigrants, demanded that the governor pardon them. That governor was Alvan T. Fuller. Fuller wasn't sure as to how to proceed, so he appointed a blue-ribbon panel to review the case. That panel was made up of the presidents of Harvard and M.I.T. and a judge of the probate court.

They reviewed the trial and the evidence and advised him that a new trial was not necessary, and he did not pardon the men. A later governor, Michael

Sacco and
Vanzetti.

Dukakis, proclaimed that they were unfairly tried but did not pardon them. Fuller took a lot of heat for his decision, and his good deeds and successes are probably clouded by that event. Certainly Sacco and Vanzetti are better recalled than he is. Fuller gave up his office at age fifty-one.

Fuller never accepted monetary compensation for his service. Known for his donations to worthy causes, he also established the Fuller Foundation. After two terms as governor, Fuller returned to business pursuits. He chaired the board of the Cadillac-Oldsmobile Corporation. In 1958, he died and was buried in Rye, New Hampshire.

But the Fuller story doesn't end there. Alvan's son, Peter, was an excellent athlete, too—an undefeated wrestler and a heavyweight boxer with an impressive record. He was also a sportsman and had a horse, Native Dancer, that won the Kentucky Derby. Peter, however, had insulted the Kentucky authorities when he donated his winnings from a previous race to Coretta Scott King upon the assassination of her husband, Dr. Martin Luther King Jr. The victory in the Kentucky Derby was shortly afterward set aside because of a dubious claim that the horse had a trace of an analgesic in its urine. Fuller won an appeal, but the appeal was then overturned by Kentucky authorities. Continuing the family sports tradition, Peter's daughter, Abby, granddaughter of Alvan, was a champion female jockey who was inducted into the Sports Hall of Fame in Boston.

The auto mile was spearheaded, then, by a Yankee or Brahmin if you will. While auto sales were not labor intensive, assembly, repair and maintenance were, and that called for people who could be readily trained to do those tasks.

# Brookline, Brighton and the Parting of Ways

The Irish presence in Boston also extended to Brighton. As they had in Brookline, Irish immigrants provided the labor for the great amount of work that had to be done in Brighton. They came in increasing numbers, reaching 40 percent before mid-century and a majority in subsequent years. In that regard it was similar to Boston and other towns with commerce and industry.

They settled close to where there was industry, especially in North Brighton and around Brighton Center. The Irish did well in labor-intensive jobs but also began their own small companies in offshoots of the livestock trade as well as running hotels and saloons. Notably, some went into politics and found out that they were good at it. By the time of the big vote on annexation, several held important town positions,

Unlike their confreres in Brookline, most of the Brighton Irish favored annexation and helped turn out a successful vote. The Irish majority also turned Brighton into the first town in Middlesex County to vote Democratic regularly. (Before annexation, Brighton was part of Middlesex, not Suffolk County.)

Another aspect of the Irish Catholic influx, along with the new and strident leadership of Cardinal O'Connell, who became archbishop in 1907, was the building of some outstanding institutions in Brighton, most of them on hilltops. The architecture was as fascinating as that fact.

The first of these was St. John's Seminary in 1881, a complex of buildings clustered around a French-style castle. Several churches were built as well, starting with St. Columbkille's on Market Street. In 1891, a school for girls and convent, Mount St. Joseph's Academy, was constructed on Cambridge Street.

In Allston, St. Anthony's Church, a Romanesque Revival–style church, was built on Holton Street, while in Brighton off Washington Street, St Gabriel's Monastery was erected in Spanish Mission style. On the same property but farther down the hill, St. Elizabeth's Hospital—in the same architectural style—rose in 1912. The year 1912 also brought the Cenacle Convent to Lake Street.

On the Commonwealth Avenue corner of Lake Street and next to the seminary, Cardinal O'Connell built a striking residence that would be the headquarters of the archdiocese. It was built in Roman style using a bequest from a wealthy Catholic, theater owner B.F. Keith.

Brighton had numerous Protestant churches as well and one Jewish temple, but the building of all these Catholic institutions in a short period was quite remarkable. Altogether, construction by the archdiocese in this turn-of-the-century period showed five churches, the seminary, three schools, a monastery, two convents and three hospitals. Few parts of Boston

St. Columbkille's Church, Market Street.

or anywhere else could boast that kind of parochial activity, but it all fit in with the new cardinal's vision, as we shall see.

Not far from Packard's Corner in Allston, and just off the auto mile, was Braves Field. The National League Boston Braves played in the South End and were 1914 world champions before moving here from 1915 to 1952. They then left Boston for Milwaukee and then Atlanta. The team won the league championship in 1948 but generally fielded poor teams. The field is now part of Boston University.

About a mile down Commonwealth Avenue and just up Brookline Avenue was Fenway Park, home of the Red Sox. It was built in 1912, and the Red Sox won the World Series that year as well as in 1915 and 1918 before vacating that title for eighty-six years. The park is due to celebrate its one hundredth anniversary in 2012. The first game ever played at Fenway went eleven innings, and the home team beat New York 7–6. The opener did not get much mention in the newspapers since they were full of details about the sinking of the *Titanic* less than a week earlier.

Another sports arena is the same age. The Skating Club of Boston on Soldiers Field Road in Allston has been home to hundreds of figure skating champions, many of whom trained there. The club is one of the few in the country that owns its own building, and despite some modernization, it remains essentially the same after one hundred years.

# Chapter 4

# *Immigration and Political Tension*

The influx of Irish immigration into Boston reached its zenith during the mid-1800s; any of them could've been potato farmers who faced starvation when the blight ruined their crops. They came to Boston and settled in crowded communities near the waterfront in the North End and East Boston, taking whatever jobs (mostly unskilled) they could find. They came in huge numbers and then in even larger numbers, overwhelming the Yankees who ran the city. Over time their labor was needed to build the new mills and roads.

Of course they needed housing, so landlords subdivided houses and rented single rooms to whole families at higher prices than they were worth. That meant that these areas where immigrants lived (like Fort Hill) were crammed with people. The small units apportioned to them usually had no running water or sanitation and often no ventilation or daylight. Not surprisingly, disease was widespread, especially cholera. Three out of five Irish children born in Boston at that time did not reach the age of six, and adults arriving in Boston would live only six more years on average.

Rowdy behavior and drunkenness were rife, as was crime. Even the few unskilled jobs available paid much more than work in Ireland had, so there was a fierce competition for jobs among the immigrants and between them and the lower-class Bostonians—who resented them. These feelings were publicly expressed in the "No Irish Need Apply" signs.

By the time of the Civil War, about one of four Bostonians was an Irish immigrant. However, during the Civil War, many of the Irish proved to be loyal Americans and brave fighters for the Union cause. Those who enlisted got bonuses, and while there were some involved in draft riots, especially in New York, others made outstanding contributions like the Massachusetts Ninth, and its Twenty-eighth Regiment served as part of the famed Irish Brigade that saw action in most of the battles on the eastern front, carrying its distinctive green flag with golden harp.

Many of those Irish who did not enlist found work in shipyards, factories and armories and made decent wages from these jobs. So the Civil War helped many Irish make a step up.

As they advanced economically, the Irish moved out of the central city, especially Fort Hill and the North End, to places like South Boston, Charlestown, Dorchester, Brighton, Brookline and West Roxbury, using horse-drawn trolleys like those of the West End Railway. These communities, with their infusion of new people, needed streets, schools, churches, hospitals and other infrastructure for which the immigrants could provide labor. They provided labor to build some of these communities close to Boston.

The Irish could also aspire to jobs in the new police and fire departments or for the public utilities—water, electric, gas and telephone. After working for others for a time, the more ambitious opened their own companies in construction trades or trucking.

One area where the Irish moved to was Brookline, which needed a labor force since it was the home mostly of wealthy business owners and professionals, none of whom was ready to do the heavy lifting. The Irish moved into two areas near Brookline Village. One, between the village and Brookline (then "Western") Avenue, was known as "The Marsh." It was an area viewed with distaste if not fear by outsiders. In reporting on a murder, the *Boston Advertiser* mentioned in its October 28, 1871 edition that the young female victim was from "the marsh, an Irish neighborhood of exceedingly bad repute, and where nightly occur drunks and rows which are a scandal to their respectable neighbors."

The reportage reveals more about attitudes toward the Irish in that day than it knows. Irish neighborhoods in Boston were viewed at least as distastefully. Similarly, in Brookline, the elite worried about decadent living conditions in this swampy area causing diseases, as well as the fact that the Irish were Roman Catholic. But they realized that a local population from the lower strata was needed to do the work they couldn't or wouldn't do. The class differences were more striking in Brookline than they would be elsewhere since Brookline had essentially no middle class as a buffer. Some of the Irish would rise to that station economically because they were in a good position in Brookline where they could find work more readily than their kinsmen who lived in Boston, and they were doing essentially all the manual labor in a town that was steadily building. In that sense, Brookline was a closed shop.

Getting involved in politics was a natural progression for the Irish in Boston, where they were becoming a majority, but it took some doing, and of course there was great resistance to it. The years following the Civil War were not good for Democrats, including the Irish and the small number of Yankee Democrats. The Republicans—the "Party of Lincoln"—held sway up until the corrupt Republican administration of Ulysses S. Grant allowed the Democrats to get some traction. Even at that, it took until 1884 for the Democrats to win the White House with Grover Cleveland.

Meanwhile a young Irishman named Patrick Collins began to organize Democrats in order to get a foothold in Massachusetts politics by way of a Yankee-Irish coalition. Patrick J. Maguire took over the leadership of the Boston Irish and decided that with their growing numbers and their spread into the various wards of Boston the Irish should be able to win the mayor's seat. And sure enough, they did. In 1884, Hugh O'Brien, a self-made businessman and fiscal conservative, won the election.

O'Brien was viewed by the Yankees as the "right sort" of Irishman. He was businesslike, accomplished, sober, respectful of others and spoke English well; he was elected to four terms as mayor. O'Brien was conservative but also had a vision of the future. One thing he foresaw was that Boston should acquire parklands before they were developed. Such land existed, especially

Patrick Collins statue on Commonwealth Avenue, Back Bay.

in West Roxbury and Hyde Park (which became part of the city in 1912). In 1938, when the New Deal's Works Progress Administration (WPA) created Stoney Brook Reservation and the public George Wright Golf Course, they fulfilled that vision.

During this time the Irish began to build a political hierarchy as other Irishmen set themselves up as "bosses" of the wards they lived in. These bosses had lieutenants, and they had their cadres and so on.

The best known of these was Martin Lomasney, ward boss of the West End's Ward 8, whose power and influence was such that he was known as the "Mahatma" (like Gandhi). He served as an alderman and was elected to the state Senate and was a four-term state legislator until 1907. However, he didn't care much for elected office, preferring to campaign for friends instead. He made it a habit to run for the legislature each third term and to promote younger protégées in between.

Usually, Martin decided upon a candidate but then waited until the last moment to reveal his choice. Those he backed usually won. People thus paid attention to what he said. One of those things was: "Never write if you can speak; never speak if you can nod; never nod if you can wink."

The Mahatma had his political tricks, of course. In one election, his candidate was facing one who was running a sticker campaign (like a write-in, but with the name preprinted on a sticker). Lomasney apparently managed to have his opponent's stickers arrive with no glue on the back so that they wouldn't stick to the ballot. However, a congressional committee that investigated awarded the election to his opponent.

At about this time, the forebears of what would become the Kennedy political dynasty came to prominence in Boston politics. John "Honey Fitz" Fitzgerald was ward boss of the North End. He was elected to the Common Council, a Boston legislative body, to the state Senate and to Congress for three terms. Then in 1906, he was elected Boston's first native-born Irish American mayor, serving until 1908 and again from 1910 to 1914.

He was called "Honey Fitz" because of his charming blarney-like gift of gab. Fitzgerald could have been an actor on the stage or an entertainer of some sort—perhaps a singer or vaudevillian. He became known as the only politician who could sing "Sweet Adeline" while sober and get away with it.

But the "show biz" aspects of politics with its hoopla and rough and tumble offered him more than any stage career could have. They called his talk "Fitzblarney" and his followers "Dearos" because he described his district as the "Dear old North End."

# Immigration and Political Tension

During his two terms, the aquarium at City Point in South Boston was built, as was the Franklin Park Zoo. However, his first administration was rife with corruption in city construction projects, and he lost a bid for reelection. A state-appointed Boston Finance Commission uncovered plenty of it and fostered the belief that Boston's politicians had to be carefully watched.

Certainly appearances were not good. City Hall was jammed with job seekers, political cronies, lobbyists, contractors and salesmen—so many for so long that the city's business was put off until after business hours. To the

"Honey Fitz."

Brahmin community, their worst fears had been realized.

Across the harbor in East Boston, Patrick J. Kennedy, or "P.J.," the son of immigrants, was a tavern owner who became well-to-do by importing whiskey. He was a ward boss and did most of his work behind the scenes. In fact, P.J. opposed Fitzgerald when he ran for mayor, but they were united in 1914 when P.J.'s son Joseph P. Kennedy married Rose Fitzgerald, the oldest daughter of the mayor. Joe and Rose were to become the parents of John, Robert and Ted Kennedy.

When he returned from World War II as a decorated hero, John F. Kennedy decided to run for Congress, and his eighty-three-year-old grandfather, Honey Fitz, helped him plan his campaign. When he won, Fitzgerald, still the showboat he had always been, danced a jig at the victory celebration, sang "Sweet Adeline" and predicted publicly that JFK would one day be president. When he reached that pinnacle, JFK renamed the presidential yacht the *Honey Fitz* in honor of his maternal grandfather.

These Irish politicians had a different view of government than the Yankees who mostly opposed and sometimes cooperated with them.

The Yankees had long looked upon government as a means of setting and enforcing rules for the public interest, a limited government that would provide men of quality and experience to become their leaders. The Irish, like other immigrant and minority groups, looked to government as an entity that could do things for them individually, to provide them with safety, the things needed for survival and for political and economic advancement. Thus, to the Yankees, the rise of the Irish in government meant a dismal future. Even worse, to them, were other immigrant groups who couldn't even speak English and had no notion of Anglo-Saxon traditions, with which at least the Irish had some familiarity.

Next to the Irish, the Italians were most numerous, arriving from southern Italy at a time when severe drought and the lack of arable soil had struck their hillside farming communities. They settled in the North End and East Boston in conclaves of people from the same towns and sections of Italy. There were also Lithuanians in the City Point area of South Boston and Polish and Russian Jews escaping persecution in those countries.

The growing power of the (mostly) Irish had another component—the rising power of the Catholic Church. There had been plenty of antagonism between the Yankee Protestants and the Irish Catholics, and some of it was religious in tone. The burning of the Ursuline Convent in Charlestown in 1834 is perhaps the most problematic example of this.

When William H. O'Connell was made archbishop of Boston in 1907 (he later was made cardinal), he took an affirmative and activist pro-Catholic stand. After strengthening the Catholic hierarchy and his power

Cardinal O'Connell.

over individual parishes, he set out to unify the Catholic community by encouraging them to take a greater part in their own religious organizations.

He also drew a sharp distinction between Catholics and non-Catholics, telling Catholics not to enter non-Catholic churches or to take part in Protestant ceremonies. He urged youth to join the CYO (Catholic Youth Organization) instead of groups such as Boy Scouts, Girl Scouts, YMCA or YWCA. Perhaps most bothersome to Protestants, he urged Catholics to attend Catholic schools and colleges, of which many were now built, and he even persuaded Mayor Fitzgerald to send his daughter Rose to the Academy of the Sacred Heart instead of Wellesley as planned. This bold initiative troubled the Yankees, in part because they viewed the public schools as a great leveler to help acculturate immigrants into the society. Now these children would be beyond their reach.

O'Connell told Boston, "The Puritan has passed. The Catholic remains."

That was true as far as population and Boston politics were concerned. However, the Yankees kept control of the state government well into the twentieth century and would control banks and business in Boston for even longer.

The Yankee strategy was to make it difficult or impossible for a Boston led by the Irish to accomplish what it wanted. One way to do this would have been to make Boston part of metropolitan efforts. It could also be put under strict state control. Both methods were tried from time to time, but for the most part the Republican-controlled state legislature tried to control Boston's political system and often succeeded.

One thing they did, as we have seen, was to appoint a watchdog Boston Finance Commission. The charter reform of 1909 was meant to weaken the power of ward bosses by giving the mayor more power. That didn't work because it depended on electing a Yankee as mayor, which seldom happened.

Most metropolitan schemes failed because outside towns didn't want to join with Boston, which they saw as corrupted by people like Fitzgerald and later Curley and the power of their ethnic group. However, the Metropolitan District Commission was formed, made up of Boston and the cities and towns around it. It controlled the banks of the Charles and Mystic Rivers, the Blue Hills and state reservations. The MDC included the previously formed Metropolitan Park Commission and Metropolitan Water and Sewerage Board. The MDC—its members appointed by the governor—had its own large police force. It was formed because of the outlying towns' distrust of Boston and its Irish mayors, especially James Michael Curley.

The conflict between these groups continued, and personalities came into play as well. It was a major reason why Boston's growth became stagnated so that when the nation entered its Great Depression at the end of 1929, Boston stayed in it longer than other places and remained in the doldrums for some time thereafter.

With all its improvements in Copley Square and Post Office Square, the city of Boston still limited itself in other ways. It put restrictions on building heights, for one thing. The legislature had imposed a restriction that said no building could be constructed that would be higher than the dome of the State House. The legislature put restrictions on special areas as well: seventy feet along the edges of parks, one hundred feet on the north side of Copley Square, ninety on the others and seventy feet in the vicinity of the State House.

After the Civil War, it became possible to build tall buildings because of improved construction methods as well as inventions like the elevator. Boston's first "skyscraper" was the thirteen-story Ames Building, which is still in use near the Old State House. The Winthrop Building of 1894 was the first in Boston built with a steel frame, an improvement that allowed the construction of much higher buildings.

In 1904, Boston put height restrictions on structures. In business areas, buildings could be 125 feet tall, whereas in residential districts they were

Ames Building, Boston.

Custom House Tower.

limited to 80 feet. The Custom House Tower was an exception since it was a federal building. When it needed to expand, the present tower was built atop its Greek classical portico, making it at 496 feet the tallest building in Boston by far. It had no rival until the first John Hancock Building was erected on Berkeley Street in the Back Bay in 1947. It was only one foot shorter than the Custom House, and the two stood out starkly among the much smaller buildings. In 1964, the Prudential Tower exceeded both.

With its self-imposed limits and inability to project a vision for its future, along with the ethnically based struggle between state and city, Boston lacked leadership to shed its garments of restraint.

It was about to have a leader who was strong and memorable, but who, in many ways, made things worse.

# Chapter 5

# *James Michael Curley and the Ethnic Struggle*

James Michael Curley is perhaps Boston's best-known mayor. He made a major impact on the city—maybe *the* major impact during the fifty years of his political career, which included four different periods as mayor.

Despite his impact, few if any know the real man. He was loved and hated in equal parts, and in fact, Faneuil Hall Marketplace has not one but two statues of him, one of him standing making a speech with his chest and stomach out in a familiar pose, the other of him sitting on a park bench and perhaps reflecting back on his long career or regretting his mistakes—although that would be out of character. The title of his autobiography was, after all, *I'd Do It Again*.

The statue of *Curley as Orator* certainly makes sense. One could say that he spent a lot of time speaking, and he was an outstanding and compelling speaker who used his voice like an instrument and could often spellbind an audience.

If he spent time thinking back on his career—unless it was in private moments of prayer, which were many—we don't know about it. His was a career worth reflection and also puzzlement. Curley was like an everyman—only more so. He was saint and sinner, visionary and narrow-minded, statesman and "pol." He saved Boston or ruined it, according to your point of view. Always entertaining, Curley was never dull.

He was thoroughly despised by the Yankee/Brahmin leadership, who were also the business and commercial leaders. The tension and hostility that lasted during Curley's roughly half-century career can certainly be seen as a major—though not the only—cause of Boston's lack of growth during the same period.

# James Michael Curley and the Ethnic Struggle

Statues of James Curley, Quincy Market.

Curley was ahead of his time in playing "the race card," but you could more truthfully call it "the ethnic card." He often complained, "I am being persecuted because of my race," by which he meant his Irish ethnicity.

Curley could count on support from the ethnic minorities of Boston and the Irish in particular. That was significant, since they accounted for nearly 40 percent of the people who lived in the city. He had a motto that appealed to working-class people: "Work harder than anyone else, preserve your self-respect and keep your word." Those things fit him, though they were far from all-inclusive and pointed to his best attributes. Others would point to his worst.

He revealed no great vision for the city of Boston. Curley was a doer, an accomplisher and a hardworking man whom his constituents were able to approach. But he didn't often make compromises in order to help the city. Coalition building did not suit him. An enemy was pretty much an enemy. In fact, he liked to tweak the noses of the Yankees and was also an effective user of sarcasm toward his political enemies of all stripes, often resorting to untruths and exaggerations in order to make his points and have his way.

It's no surprise, then, that he was generally disliked by his political peers and had few friends, but he did connect with his constituents, many of whom were loyal for life. Curley became a polished speaker by taking lessons and practicing his delivery. He highlighted his speeches with Shakespearean or classical references, learned mainly while reading everything in the library of the Charles Street Jail, where he was imprisoned early in his career. (He spent time in jail on two different occasions, but it seemed to have no negative effect on his ability to get elected.)

On the other hand, his training in speaking had a definite positive affect. He attended the Staley College of the Spoken Word in Brookline Village (where Olympia Brown of Weymouth, the first American female pastor, also trained), but Curley also did a lot of homework, training himself to have a mellifluous voice with a range of tones.

The school's founder, Delbert Staley, said years later, "He had the harsh Boston voice and the vocabulary of a fishmonger. But I straightened out his grammar, gave him a vocabulary and trained his voice." But Curley's "homework" counted for something. He was a student of public speaking, learning from such men as William Jennings Bryan and Billy Sunday. As a result, you'd be more impressed if you heard Curley's speeches than if you read them.

Curley made many enemies in his long career. While others might enjoy getting into fistfights, Curley preferred to use verbal attacks. He enjoyed verbal assaults on the Boston Brahmins, and these were sincere since he encouraged his Irish constituents to blame their woes on the Yankees. Those constituents added their own voices to the attacks. And all this had an effect.

Many of the so-called Brahmins who had long dominated the city came to feel unwelcome in Boston. The exodus of Protestants to the suburbs that took place during the Curley era left a lasting legacy. They had been major taxpayers and ran most of the businesses. While they often kept the businesses, many moved to places like Brookline, where they could help make the rules and build a town that suited them. Curley accused these people of trying to escape from the problems of the city and called it "a geography of avoidance." However, living in Brookline or Newton, they could not vote against him.

Curley resented even what remained of Yankee influence in the city, especially the attempts at reform by the good government committees and the ability of the state to monitor and control city finances and corruption. This resentment no doubt stemmed from the treatment past and present of the Irish at the hands of the Yankees who looked down on even the most accomplished of them.

Curley's immediate goal was to provide relief for Boston's poorer citizens, particularly the Irish. He found jobs for them, especially in big public works programs, did favors and always listened. To him, a person's ethnicity and background were what counted most. However, as he told one critic, he would rather spend the public money on jobs and work projects than on welfare. But in so doing, he helped to divide the city, not unite it. To some extent these harmful divisions remained for many years after he was gone. Boston and its suburbs might have worked cooperatively in regional efforts that would have benefited all of them, but the bitter relationship and mistrust made this quite difficult. At one point during the depression Curley suggested regional cooperation, but it was not taken seriously. His political opponents did not believe they could work with him.

Another problem with Curley's political glad-handing was that his largesse also came from public funds and put the city in bad financial straits. He often overspent the budget, and during his years the city usually ran in the red. This was during a period of economic hardship and even depression, a time when the city desperately needed to be set in a new direction. Here is where he obviously fell short. He could not lift Boston out of depression or give it the spark of leadership it needed while it settled into the doldrums, as it did during most of his years.

Rather, he feuded with business interests, raising their taxes and inflating their assessments—particularly if they opposed him, as did the *Boston Herald*, whose assessment he did, in fact, raise after it opposed the tunnel to East Boston. Curley became known for his public works. You can still find his name on many things in Boston. He built things in the neighborhoods that supported him, things like parks and playgrounds, swimming pools and sidewalks. They sprang up in the outlying neighborhoods, where his supporters lived, not in the downtown, an area that he allowed to deteriorate.

While he built schools in Roxbury or Jamaica Plain, he let the docks on Atlantic Avenue fall into the ocean and the sidewalks on Beacon Hill fall apart. He may have been, as he said, a man of the people, but that did not mean all of the people, just those he deemed deserving of his handouts.

One story is almost iconic in its portrayal of Curley as the savior of the poor and downtrodden. When he became mayor and saw the dirty condition of City Hall, he ordered it cleaned up. But when he saw the Irish cleaning women down on their knees scrubbing the floor of City Hall as a result of his directive, it reminded him of how the Irish women—like his own mother—had to always be on their knees scrubbing floors in Yankee households. He decreed that long-handled mops would be used at City Hall and that no cleaning woman would scrub floors while on her knees again. He declared that a woman should go down on her knees only when praying to God.

Unspoken in this iconic tale is the concept that he ameliorated the condition of some people but did not really do anything that would advance them from those things that put them in that condition to start with. There was often a handout without a hand up.

His chosen enemies fought back. While the Yankees controlled the state legislature, they handcuffed Boston by limiting its (and Curley's) ability to exercise home rule. Boston and only Boston could not raise taxes without state approval, which gave the state a chokehold on city growth. Mayors also could not appoint the police commissioner or the licensing board. The struggle lasted for decades.

His attitudes were formed from his early days in Roxbury. His father, a day laborer, made a bet with a coworker that he could lift a four-hundred-pound curbstone. He won the bet but died from the effort. Curley's mother, now a widow with two young sons, had to get along without help from the community bosses, working at menial jobs while Jim helped by taking part-time jobs.

As a student at Roxbury's Dearborn School, young Jim was noted for his speaking skills and his eagerness to learn. Though he worked hard at school, he had to balance his schoolwork with those part-time jobs. His days were long.

When he got older, he replaced the ward boss of the area he lived in and began his run for municipal and state offices, holding two posts in the city and then in the state legislature from 1902 to 1903. He had been elected a city alderman while serving a term in jail for taking a postal test for a friend. He turned this setback around with the slogan, "He did it for a friend."

From 1911 to 1913, he served in Congress and then decided to run for mayor of Boston, even though the current mayor, "Honey Fitz" Fitzgerald, appeared ready to run for reelection. Curley put a stop to this with one of his patented dirty tricks. He announced publicly that he planned to give three lectures, one of which would be called "Great Lovers from Cleopatra to Toodles." "Toodles" Ryan was a shapely blonde and very young cigarette girl (about the age of Fitzgerald's daughter) whose name had been linked with the mayor. Rather than submit himself and his family to scandal, Fitzgerald withdrew from the race, and Curley defeated the other candidates. The Kennedy family, of which Honey Fitz was a forebear, would never forget this.

To win, Curley actually had to run against the Democratic machine in Boston, which just wasn't done. The machine was Irish to the core, including the fabled Martin Lomasney and most of the other ward bosses. The Yankees, who might have backed someone else, instead pretty much sat this one out, and to their later regret, Curley won by a small margin.

Curley proved himself to be a maverick, breaking with the Democratic machine in Boston as he had and running against its current champion. The maverick status was not new. He had run against the candidate of his local ward boss Maguire earlier, probably because Maguire was not helping the people and had not helped his mother after his father died when he was ten. He was also a different kind of Irish mayor—the first to openly attack the Yankee community and flout their cultural values. Previous Irish mayors had attempted to get along with the business interests to some extent, but not Curley. He made fun of their institutions such as Harvard and Beacon Hill.

He wrote to a member of the Harvard Board of Overseers:

> *The Massachusetts of the Puritans is as dead as Caesar, but there is no need to mourn the fact. Their successors—the Irish—had letters and learning, culture and civilization when the ancestors of the Puritans were savages running half-naked through the forests of Britain. It took the Irish to make Massachusetts a fit place to live in.*

It's no surprise that the rich hated him, and he returned the favor. He once proposed selling Public Garden and making the Common a pumping station, just to show disrespect for the traditions of the Brahmins who loved those places. He had no use for these downtown green spaces and would have traded them for playgrounds in Roxbury or Dorchester or a bathhouse in South Boston on L Street (all of which, people believed, would have given him kickbacks from contractors).

So Curley had enemies on both sides, among the Irish and most of the Yankees, at whom he thumbed his nose. Rather than try to get along with

Curley, the Yankees learned that they'd do better allying with an Irish American they could work with—sort of the lesser of two evils.

After he was elected to a second term that began in 1922, the Yankee-controlled state legislature passed a law preventing the mayor of Boston from succeeding himself. Most historians believe that the law was aimed squarely at Curley, and he thought so, too. That did not prevent him from winning a third term in 1929 or a fourth in 1945 while under indictment for mail fraud. Altogether he ran for mayor ten times.

Curley was not reelected in 1918, when all his enemies lined up against him and allowed the election of Andrew James Peters, whom Curley referred to as "the Brookline squire who was endowed with three apostolic names."

His names were not the least of Peters's troubles. When the Boston police went on strike in 1919, he delayed in calling on the state for help. When Governor Calvin Coolidge sent the state militia, it was he who was credited with breaking the strike and it helped his political fortunes. Peters's reputation was later tarred by his affair with a young woman with the improbable name of Starr Faithfull. The story of this beautiful woman and her mysterious death on a Long Island beach later was used by writer John O'Hara as a plot in his novel *Butterfield 8*, also a film starring Elizabeth Taylor. Peters tried to become governor in 1920 but was not nominated.

Curley tried a different route. After he failed to get reelected in 1918, he ran unsuccessfully for Congress in 1920; thus, he was out of the mayor's office during the two major events of 1919 in Boston, one of which gained national attention and had political ramifications. These were the Molasses Flood and the Boston Police Strike.

Governor Calvin Coolidge sent armed militia to stem the strike and gained national notoriety for himself when he proclaimed: "There is no right to strike against the public safety by anybody, anywhere, any time."

This struck a resonant chord with a public fearful of unlawful activity and signs of radicalism that were taking hold. Most strikes in that era failed, but what was called the Red Scare continued and manifested itself again in Boston during the trial of the radicals Sacco and Vanzetti. Coolidge was put on the Republican ticket for vice president under Warren Harding.

Harding's administration addressed the recession of 1920 that had been brought on by the Progressive Woodrow Wilson and brought the country out of it. His term ended with his death in 1923, at which time Coolidge became the first Massachusetts president since the Adamses. He continued the policies of his predecessor, but without the corruption he had displayed. He managed to repair the reputation to the government and reduced both taxes and the debt.

If Curley had been mayor or governor during the police strike, he would not likely have been boosted politically as Coolidge was. The year was ripe for a Republican victory just as 1932 would be for the Democrats.

Curley also favored the striking police, who were mostly fellow Irish Bostonians. Years later he said that had he been mayor, there would have been no strike. Coolidge would have had to wait for another propitious moment.

James Curley.

Curley had done better sticking to local politics for now. So in 1921 Curley ran for mayor yet again, winning by a narrow margin. During this term (1922–24) he upgraded Boston City Hospital, adding buildings, including a fourteen-story maternity building. He also built twenty health facilities throughout the city.

He also, during this term, changed the swampy mudflats of South Boston into a milelong Strandway and built the L Street Bathhouse at a cost of $350,000, which, he said, "provides the poor with all the comforts of a Florida trip." He did take people off welfare and gave them public jobs, saying, "I can give a man a city job at, say, $15 a week, or I can put him on the welfare at $12 a week. Giving him the job helps him to preserve his self-respect, and that, I think, is worth the extra three dollars."

However, he spent so much on civic improvements, and most people believed he took kickbacks for himself, that he didn't even have enough money to pay the city employees. He had to borrow against future taxes. Curley's taxing and spending policies had discouraged investment in the city and gained him the hostility of the business community. However, his policies weren't the only harmful ones. Federal housing policies (including the later G.I. Bill), along with suburban highway construction, gave people reasons to move to the suburbs, where they could get a mortgage from the government and where new roads could take them in and out of the city where many still worked. This more rapid suburbanization and the loss of tax dollars that left with these people hurt the city by taking away energetic young people as well.

Of those suburbanites who still worked in the city, many brought their cars and added to traffic and parking problems at the same time they were being critical of the city government—a government that lacked sufficient home rule to fix those problems. The state even limited its ability to borrow money to pay for those improvements.

Curley would have liked to get rid of the Finance Committee and the MDC and regain the mayor's right to pick his own police commissioner. These were among the ways in which the state had stymied the city. But they had done this mainly because of Curley, many would have said.

Transportation continued to be a concern. Getting in and out of the city to the suburbs was one thing. Going farther afield took ships, trains or planes. It was only in the third decade of the twentieth century that Boston took a major step toward providing aviation to and from the core city.

The East Boston section of the city has played a major role in the transportation with construction of the East Boston Tunnel in 1904 for trains, Sumner Tunnel (1934), Callahan Tunnel (1959) and Ted Williams Tunnel (1997) for ground vehicles and, of course the airport, which started as "Boston Airport" in 1923 in the part of East Boston known as Jeffries Point and its small airstrip, Jeffery Field.

In 1924, Curley made his first run for governor of the state. His opponent was Alvan T. Fuller, whose story is told elsewhere in these pages. Fuller, a Progressive Republican, was an honorable man, but he had the boldness to, in Curley's own words, "make the word 'Curleyism' sound like a communicable disease."

Curley's own definition would not have been hotly disputed by a Progressive. He said Curleyism was "a kindly, considerate, humane treatment of the poor, the sick and the unfortunate." That much would have been fair political give and take, but Curley went on to call Fuller the "Klan candidate." The Ku Klux Klan, never big in New England, was just then mounting a resurgence based on an exposé in a New York newspaper, and a few fringe members were burning crosses in Massachusetts.

Curley called attention to these crosses and probably spread this deviltry by doing so. Fuller accused Curley of sparking them. Some speculated that his followers were doing so, but in any case the issue burned itself out just as the crosses did. Fuller was elected, but Curley gained enough votes to encourage him to try again later.

In 1928, Curley campaigned vigorously for Al Smith, playing a major role in Smith's narrow Bay State win that did not reflect his national standing in a loss to Herbert Hoover.

James Michael Curley often found revenge sweet. Just before the 1929 election, on a radio show, he blasted a school committeewoman who had spoken out against him. She was a popular volunteer, as well as a wife and mother, and his diatribe cost him many votes, although he managed to just eke out a win. Curley was known as a man who got back at his enemies.

# Chapter 6

# *National Politics and the Great Depression*

James Michael Curley's dealings with national politicians often returned fewer benefits than he had hoped for. As we have seen, during the 1928 race for the Democratic nomination, he—like the rest of the Democrats in Massachusetts—backed New York governor Alfred E. Smith—"The Happy Warrior," as he was known. Smith won the nomination on the third ballot at the Democratic national convention and became the first Catholic candidate to run for president on a major party ticket. Smith was also opposed to the prohibition of alcohol, pitting him against the "drys" who were trying to put an end to drinking and drunkenness. Those two factors, as well as the good economy, probably worked against Smith. He lost handily to Herbert C. Hoover, who continued the string of Republican presidents, which—broken only by Wilson—reached back into the nineteenth century.

Four years later, the country was deep into the Great Depression. This time around, the presidential race would be a different story for the Democrats and for Curley, one with steep downturns for him. On the return from a trip to Europe, he caught a train from New York and found that he was on the same train as Franklin Delano Roosevelt (FDR). Curley, alert to any political possibility, sent his card over to FDR. They had a chat and got to know each other. According to Curley, FDR asked for his support and promised Curley a spot in his cabinet or an equivalent post in return. Curley said he'd work for him but didn't see how he could beat Smith in Massachusetts.

Curley was never a good planner, and this didn't work out the way he hoped it would. Curley attended a luncheon at the home of Colonel House,

FDR and Al Smith.

advisor of Woodrow Wilson, where Curley told reporters that FDR would be the man to nominate for president. When that shocking remark appeared in the morning papers, Curley's stock in the state dropped like a falling elevator. Democrats turned their backs on him.

Curley got his own backup and campaigned for FDR in Massachusetts, while nearly all of the rest of the Democrats backed Smith. FDR's goal was to win the nomination without dividing the party. The Democrat who could do this would easily defeat Hoover in this Depression year. FDR lost to Smith in Massachusetts but secured the nomination at the convention.

Curley attended, although he had not been chosen as a delegate for Massachusetts. He wasn't even sure that those running the convention would let him in. While there, the wily Curley managed to become a delegate for Puerto Rico (then called "Porto Rico"). He even managed to second FDR's nomination from the floor and suggested later that he had helped arrange a shift of delegate votes that put FDR over the top. Bostonians admired his chutzpah. His popularity in his home state rose again as quickly as it had fallen.

His mayoral duties now took a back seat as he campaigned for FDR. He was scheduled to make a short campaign film for him in New York, but when he arrived at the studio, he realized he had forgotten his script. That bothered those who were running the event, but it didn't bother him. He told them he'd be even better without a script. It turned out that he was right. He winged it, and critics said it was one of the best pieces of political propaganda they had ever heard. The speech was mostly about "the forgotten man," a common theme of his in that period.

Following that, he went on a forty-one-day tour of key cities around the country, making 140 speeches in the West and Midwest, for which the Democratic Party paid nothing. Curley had mortgaged his Jamaica Plain home for $25,000 to pay for the trip. (This was the Dutch colonial Curley had built opposite Jamaica Pond, with shamrocks in its shutters. Critics wondered how he could pay for it on his limited salary, and it was mentioned for years in that regard, giving it another symbolic representation.)

Curley's trip drew big crowds and a lot of support for FDR, all of which gave him the right to feel that FDR owed him one. FDR won the presidency, of course, but there was no payoff for Curley. He was told by FDR's son, James Roosevelt, that his secretary of the navy goal was a no-go. With that hope fading, he then campaigned for an Italian ambassadorship but wound up only with an offer of ambassador to Poland—which he refused. His relationship with FDR was headed downhill, but he kept that fact away from his constituents. A politician without "pull" is a weaker person.

Boston did get Federal Housing Association money for Old Colony Village in South Boston, later called the Mary Ellen McCormick project, but not a lot more. The Boston Housing Authority (BHA) created projects in Charlestown, East Boston, South Boston and at Mission Hill, Lenox Street and Orchard Park in Roxbury.

His third term came during the Depression, and to Curley, dealing with the Depression essentially meant providing relief to the poor. His plans to lower the number of unemployed and to improve the local economy were held back, however, because the state imposed such limits on the city. That stemmed from Curley's own intransigence in dealing with the state and the city's business interests, but not entirely. The other side was partly to blame, too, and Boston got little help from the state and not much from the federal government. In 1930, for example, $10 million in federal funds went to Massachusetts, but none of this went to its capital city.

So Curley's ideas for an activist government were shot down by the state, and his building projects did not get state or federal backing. Curley had told everyone that he had an inside track with FDR, but every time he announced that he was pursuing or was getting federal money for this public project or that one, nothing came of it. He had no inside track. It would be closer to say he was anathema to FDR and his advisors.

Failure to get Boston out of its financially woeful situation was certainly not entirely Curley's fault. There were also national factors, such as the loss of industry, lack of trade and a falling stock market.

In fact, in October 1929, the Boston Stock Exchange had lost more than a quarter of its value in just two days. By July 1932, the stock market had lost almost 90 percent of its value. This hit the companies of the state directly. Manufacturing cities like Lawrence, Lowell, Worcester and Fall River had already laid off workers and now had no capital to invest, and the shoemaking towns also had to close factories and lay off workers.

As the Depression reached its depths in 1934, a quarter of the state's workers were without jobs, and most had been unemployed for a year or more. Smaller factories that supplied the larger ones closed, too. Families lost their homes and were evicted from their rentals, moving in together into crowded tenements. People struggled to get enough to eat. Some even had to eat out of garbage cans. A falling spirit and an attitude of depression also pressed down upon Boston.

In fact, during the Depression, Curley appeared to be depressed himself, at least politically. After his rough treatment and disappointment as a result of the Roosevelt campaign and his failure to get an appointment that he thought suited him, some of his feistiness and his own peculiar kind of idealism seemed to dissipate. While FDR was putting his New Deal into action, Curley—cut from a similar cloth—did not put his heart into getting all he could from it for his "people."

Jack Beatty views Curley's actions during this period more harshly. In his book *The Rascal King*, he charges that Curley abandoned people in need, the very ones he always claimed were "his people." Doing that was even worse, he said, than his graft or his ethnic polarizing, which were his means of gaining power—though dubious means.

Beatty, and those who agree with him, would say that being a "Robin Hood" was a political affliction and harmful to the good of the city, but at least it was an honest way of being dishonest. However, when he was doing these social goods for his own benefit, he was simply a crook.

But let's let Beatty say it for himself:

> *By using that power for good—good defined in basic terms: a job for a man down on his luck, a bed in the City Hospital, the building of a neighborhood health clinic, the installation of a solarium on the beach at South Boston, the dollar bill slipped to the wino, with no temperance lecture attached—by such actions, at least partially he wiped the moral slate clean. "He may have been a crook, but he was our crook"—that claim justified him.*

Beatty goes on to say, "But like many politicians, holding office had become an end in itself for Curley; as the following months made clear he had come to care more about power than about its purpose."

Beatty can give evidence that supports his point. Curley was always feuding with New Deal officials, and that got in the way of Boston's collecting all the federal aid it could have. Boston was eligible for 22,800 jobs under the Public Works Administration (PWA), but it only filled 12,500. Beatty concludes that Curley wanted federal money, but mainly so that he could spread it out to his favorite contractors and get his kickbacks. "Men and women with families to feed did not get jobs because Curley wanted to get his first."

Those with any degree of sophistication know that appearances count—often more than facts or deeds. Symbolically, while the poor were suffering, the mayor took long European trips, three of them in three years. Public officials who take expensive vacations while the people are suffering usually suffer politically, as we can see, even by observing the public criticism that comes in our own times for officials who wine too widely on the public dime or squander their time instead of doing their jobs.

Curley ran for governor in 1934, but the Democratic Convention in Worcester nominated instead Charles C. Cole, who had been a brigadier general in France during World War I. Undeterred, Curley attacked the convention as crooked and challenged Cole in the primary and won. He then bested Gaspar Bacon in the general election and became the first Democratic mayor of Boston to become governor of Massachusetts.

In reality, Curley won partly because of a third candidate and didn't do as well as the rest of the ticket. Many of his inaugural proposals were meant to remove the boot of the state from the neck of Boston's mayor. The best example is the abolition of the hated Finance Commission, which only recently had been looking into the graft of the third Curley administration in Boston.

To stinging criticism, Curley was able to derail the commission by giving one of its Republican members a job, replacing him with a Democrat and getting control of it.

He was now in a position to do something else he'd always wanted as mayor: to allow the mayor of Boston to appoint the police commissioner. But he didn't want to give that privilege to the present mayor, Fred Mansfield, who despised him because he had given the Irish a bad name. He also did not abolish the State Tax Appeal Board, a move that would have helped overtaxed Bostonians. Instead he loaded it with patronage appointees, including his own brother.

So, having gained a position where he could at last have helped Boston, Curley chose to help himself.

In his first months as governor, Curley's vilification of his enemies and his high-handed methods, such as replacing qualified people with political hangers-on, drew negative editorial opinions, like this one from the *Springfield Union:* "Governor Curley appears to be suffering now from delusions of grandeur and sees himself becoming dictator of the Commonwealth a la Huey Long" (the populist and powerful Louisiana senator who wanted to redistribute wealth and who was also an enemy of FDR and others).

Curley's two years as governor were summed up by historian Robert McElvaine this way: "All in all, during Curley's two years in office the General Court (Legislature)…abandoned a good deal of its one time conservative aversion to large scale government spending…in response to the proddings of an aggressive governor and the whip of a persistent economic crisis."

The Sumner Tunnel opened between Boston and East Boston under Boston Harbor during Curley's term as governor. He had long favored such a tunnel, but he had wanted it to be two lanes in each direction. However, the funding only allowed two lanes within a single tube. As Curley predicted, they would come to regret this lack of foresight, and in 1961 a second (Callahan) tunnel provided the two additional lanes.

This matched the way the crisis was handled elsewhere, including inside the New Deal. While FDR introduced numerous changes and measures meant to alleviate unemployment, the results fell far short of what history seems to recall.

By 1938, employment still hovered around 20 percent in a second recession that followed the Great Depression. When the Gallup poll in 1939 asked, "Do you think the attitude of the Roosevelt administration toward business is delaying business recovery?" the American people responded "yes" by a margin of more than two to one. The super-production of World War II sent unemployment in 1943 plunging to 2 percent.

Curley also received a shower of brickbats for his personal spending of public funds while in office. People were suffering. Unemployment was rampant, but Curley didn't seem to notice, or if he did, he did not help.

The textile industry had been moving to southern locales where taxes and salaries were lower, and the shoe industry was losing market share to foreign makers. Unemployment in Bay State manufacturing cities was at all-time highs. The fishing industry, long a mainstay of Boston, had shrunk and had now moved from the decaying Atlantic Avenue section to the shores of South Boston.

In Curley's youth, an unspoken alliance had been maintained between the Irish Catholics and Yankee Protestants, one that held through most of the rest of the century. During that time, Yankee Protestant Democrats approved or supplied the mayors.

Curley, however, dug down and located the repressed bitterness that had been laid aside by the Irish and that had lain dormant during those years. It was a resentment borne of the neglect of the British during the potato famine in Ireland, which had not been caused by them, but whose effects they had done nothing to allay. A long history of antagonism between English and Irish in the British Isles still smoldered.

That long-held hostility had been reinforced in the Irish who came to Boston and experienced second-class citizenship and a Yankee population that held them at arm's length. Moreover, the Irish saw the Yankees as hypocrites for opposing slavery with their abolitionism while ignoring the suffering of a minority right in their backyard.

Curley had experienced these attitudes firsthand and understood the depths of Irish animosity. He was able to speak for the disaffected better than anyone else and did so for half a century. He did little to promote unity, and it was only as he passed from the political scene that harmony began to slowly swirl among the poisoned waters, and cooperation just then started to seep in.

His biographer, Jack Beatty, described the enmity of the Irish Americans:

> *It would be what lent them the sullen psychology of an aggrieved minority long after they had become a majority. It would be the burden of grievance that Curley's generation, under his leadership, would, in Jesse Jackson's words, "look back to pick up," and that would prevent them from going forward.*

# National Politics and the Great Depression

Curley may have been a good Christian in the sense of doing kindnesses to his fellow man (even though he may have used taxpayer funds to do it). But he was not a statesman or visionary who would lead the poor person out of his poverty. He provided fish but never thought to teach the skill of fishing.

Melvin Holli, in his *The American Mayor*, gave reasons why Curley's name belonged on the list of the worst American mayors in history:

> *A worst-list without Boston's "lovable scoundrel" Mayor J. Michael Curley (1914–17, 1922–25, 1930–33, 1946–49), also known as the "last-hurrah mayor," would be like corned beef without cabbage on St. Patrick's Day. Twice jailed, the unstoppable Curley made more political comebacks than a dying opera diva. A masterful and cynical exploiter of his own people's poverty, he inflamed the ethno-cultural conflict of his city and turned Boston city politics into a three-ring circus for half a century.*
>
> *Although, as his biographer Jack Beatty shows, Curley grossly enriched himself at public expense and lived far beyond the means of an honest public servant, financial self-aggrandizement was not really what Curley was about. Curley lived for politics and loved coming in first, no matter which office or honor he ran for. He undoubtedly would have resented coming in fourth-worst in a ten-person field, had he lived to see this expert survey.*

His years as governor being generally viewed as disastrous, Curley decided to run instead for U.S. senator in 1936. His opponent was Henry Cabot Lodge Jr., who defeated him roundly.

While he had been governor, Boston's mayor was Fred Mansfield, a different kind of Irishman. During the Mansfield administration, the city built a new City Hospital building, the George Wright Golf Course and seven schools, but overall his years were known for their austerity. Since Mansfield could not succeed himself due to the earlier ordinance, Curley tried to become mayor again in 1937 but lost to his own protégé, Maurice Tobin, who would go on to become governor and then U.S. secretary of labor.

Tobin was helped considerably by a "November Surprise" in the *Boston Post*. Election day fell on All Soul's Day, when many Catholics were attending Mass. As they left, they were handed free copies of the paper by Tobin supporters. It ran an eight-column, bold-type piece with a banner that said, "Voters of Boston," and read:

*Cardinal O'Connell, in speaking to the Catholic Alumni Association, said, "The walls are raised against honest men in civic life." You can break down those walls by voting for an honest, clean, competent young man, Maurice J. Tobin, today. He will redeem the city and take it out of the hands of those who have been responsible for graft and corruption. Maurice Tobin can win with the help of those who have had enough of these selfish old-timers. Too long they have been supported by the taxpayers. They have had more than enough.*

The cardinal's remark had been taken from an earlier speech that was not about Curley or Tobin. But many gave the story credit for Tobin's twenty-five-thousand-vote victory.

Curley decided to try for governor again in 1938, and he looked to have a lead over Leverett Saltonstall. A liberal Republican, Saltonstall had gained admirers on Beacon Hill in his years there. Though he was a Yankee, descended from a long line of them, his long, dour face gave him the look of an Irishman, as people often said. Curley made the mistake of trying to make a joke out of this, one that revealed more hostility than humor. He said: "The only reason Saltonstall advances for why he should be elected Governor, is that he has a South Boston face. This is a colossal stupidity. If he ever walked down the streets of South Boston with that face, he would be put in the hospital within a hundred yards."

Saltonstall capitalized on this faux pas, saying, "I am proud of that South Boston face. It's not a double face. It's the only one I have and it will be the same face after the election." According to local legend, Saltonstall went to South Boston, walking the streets and greeting people. He was elected.

Curley ran again for mayor in 1941 against Tobin. Tobin, true to his word, had cut spending during his four years as mayor (the term had been changed again). However, he had not reduced taxes very much. Curley, meanwhile, had been tarred with charges of corruption. But choosing between someone who had run a clean and frugal administration and one who reeked of corruption and was known for freewheeling spending, the citizens of Boston found that they had a difficult choice. They elected Tobin, but it was very close.

Curley, who never felt comfortable out of office and didn't seem to care what office it was, ran for Congress in the Eleventh District in 1942. He won and was reelected in 1944, though he didn't serve all of his second term.

Still, no one had been able to get Boston out of its depressed state. A contest was even held in 1944 by architect William Roger Greeley. He told an audience that Boston had not had the advantage of destruction by bombing that London had seen, that would have allowed it to clear out the old city for the new. The winner, a team from Harvard, said that the metropolitan area had decayed because "its vitality has not been the common concern of all those having a stake in it." It spoke about the way businesses had left the city, of its winding streets and lack of highways. They proposed a metropolitan solution but found no takers.

When Tobin was elected governor in 1945, the remaining year of his term was completed by the president of the city council, John Kerrigan. Curley decided to forego the rest of his congressional term and run again for mayor. He had some help in making that decision. Curley was deeply in debt, to the tune of $100,000 or more.

At the same time, Joseph P. Kennedy had a son about to come home from the war who needed a job—a position from which to launch a political career as directed by his father. Joseph P.'s son Joe was to have been the politician, but his death in a heroic air mission had silenced that hope, and now Joe Sr. pinned his hope on his second son, John.

Joe and Curley had a conversation. Even though Curley and the Kennedys had been longtime enemies, Joe Kennedy was willing to pay off Curley's debt and also finance his run for mayor of Boston—if he were willing to vacate his Eleventh District seat and give Joe's son a chance. So the deal was done.

By this time, the Boston newspapers were anti-Curley.

To quote Jack Beatty:

> *Kennedy's money enabled Curley to mount a radio campaign—his only alternative, since he would get no help from the newspapers, which, having lost all pretense of objectivity as far as Curley was concerned, would*

JFK, Joe Kennedy and Honey Fitz.

*promote his opponents and ignore him. Moreover, fewer and fewer people went to rallies by this time. Radio was the only way to get his message out. He would win this one on his voice or not at all.*

Fortunately for Curley, William Reilly, an opponent who could have caused him problems, had some of his own. In November 1942, a fire at the Coconut Grove nightclub had killed nearly five hundred people, and an investigation had found many violations of the fire code. Reilly had been fire commissioner, and Mayor Tobin had narrowly avoided being indicted for taking bribes from the club's owner. The fire became a campaign issue.

Reilly had said this about Curley: "Mr. Curley's public career was practically coincident with the period of Boston's decline, and I doubt whether that is just a coincidence."

Curley, nonetheless, then defeated Kerrigan, who had become his main opponent, in 1945 and began his fourth term as mayor at age seventy-one. In his inaugural address, he promised to address the drabness of Boston with an ambitious public works program financed by a loan from the state legislature of $10 million. The program would include taking down the elevated rapid transit, building a new bridge across the Charles and constructing a parking garage under Boston Common.

He also asked the legislature to declare a moratorium on appeals to the tax court. That would mean he could cut taxes on residents while raising them on businesses. The *Herald* said: "He proposes to make the property owners in downtown Boston pay for excessive valuations or even add to them." This was the same old neighborhood versus downtown class warfare he had engaged in for years. It was a reason the state wouldn't give him a free hand.

He could not begin his program because he had a criminal charge against him, which led to a trial in Washington, D.C. He had good news and bad news. The jury deliberated long into the night, and Curley had to cancel his airline reservations in order to stay for the verdict. The flight that he canceled crashed and killed everyone on board.

The charge was for mail fraud, but it had little to do with that. A swindler had used his name to gain government contracts. Curley had agreed to the use of his name, but it seems clear that he, too, was conned, and he received little if anything from the dealings.

The jury found him guilty of ten of the fourteen counts on which he'd been indicted. He faced a possible sentence of forty-seven years. But he was actually sentenced to a term of six to eighteen months in the federal penitentiary in Danbury, Connecticut.

# National Politics and the Great Depression

The rest of the Massachusetts congressional delegation (except JFK) petitioned President Truman to pardon him. Curley served five months. Then Truman commuted his sentence, later pardoning him. William Bulger, in his book on Curley, makes a compelling case that JFK was acting out of revenge—a common theme in politics—when he chose not to join the rest of the Massachusetts congressmen in appealing to Truman to pardon Curley. JFK may have recalled viscerally that Curley had stood in the way of both his grandparents, driving Honey Fitz from office and effectively ending his political career. Kennedy was close to his grandfather and probably took this chance to get even.

While Curley was in prison, city clerk John B. Hynes served as temporary mayor. Hynes was not thought to have political ambitions, but just to make sure, he was promised a large pay increase and a position for life when he returned to his job as clerk, but both would be lost if he ran for mayor.

Hynes stayed away from some major decisions, leaving those for Curley's return. Most of these involved signing contracts (for which Curley would customarily take a kickback). When he did come back, after a long first day where he put in a lot of work, mostly signing those contracts, he told reporters, "I have accomplished more in one day than has been done in the five months of my absence."

Add this to a still-growing list of Curley faux pas that had come back to haunt him politically. Hynes's family had never seen him as livid as he was that day when he returned home from City Hall. His was a long, slow burn, and it transformed him from a man with no political ambitions to a man who decided to get his revenge by becoming a contender during the 1949 election. Curley had no one but himself to blame for this nor for the towering mass of tinder that Hynes could enflame based on Curley's years of doing similar insensitive things and gathering enemies.

Hynes used this kindling. He built a coalition of supporters from various ethnic groups who had been disaffected from Curley, including college students organized by a young man named Jerome Rappaport, from women's groups and even from Republicans who viewed him as the lesser of two evils.

Even some second- and third-generation Irish realized that Curley's politics of division and social activism had given them some of the things they wanted but had not advanced them socially. Irish political power had not translated into an upwardly mobile class in Boston (unlike some Irish who had moved to places like Brookline and gone into business for themselves or had become professionals and had built careers for themselves).

Real estate taxes in Boston were the highest of any city in the country. Some fifty thousand people lived in public housing. It also spent more than the rest on welfare, police and fire and on hospitals. And City Hospital had a miserable record. In its maternity wing, 65 percent of the premature babies died soon after birth, and the death rate overall had risen by 27 percent in the last five years. The place was staffed with many patronage jobs, and even the nursing corps had gotten a bad reputation.

Curley called Hynes "a little city clerk" and joked that "Johnny can have my job anytime. Whenever I quit."

Hynes wouldn't have to wait for that. Running on the slogan "A New Boston," Hynes prevailed by carrying the outlying districts like Brighton and Allston, Hyde Park, Dorchester and West Roxbury. Curley ran again in 1951 and 1955 but was defeated both times by Hynes. He did not, however, disappear from the scene. Edwin O'Connor published *The Last Hurrah* in 1956, a fictionalized version of Curley's life, which later became a motion picture with Spencer Tracy playing the Irish politician who was the key character.

At first Curley threatened to sue O'Connor but then decided it was in his interest to embrace the bestseller. He even tried to capitalize on its fame by having his own biography ghostwritten. *I'd Do It Again* gives a friendly version of his life but reveals as much as it hides.

Curley's life had been a hard one despite his fame. He had lost his first wife and seven of his nine children—two of them on the same day while talking on the same phone at different moments. He had no close personal friends but thousands of loyal followers.

James Michael Curley passed from political life in November 1958 only because he passed from life itself. When his son and daughter had died on the same day, fifty thousand people had come to his home on the Jamaicaway. But one million people lined the streets of Boston to watch the passing of his funeral procession. He was gone but not forgotten.

# Chapter 7

# *John B. Hynes and the Spirit of Change*

There was a feeling in the air in 1949 that change was coming. The Red Sox had lost the American League pennant to the hated Yankees on the last day of the season, but hope was not extinguished. By November the city had a chance to elect a new mayor whose name was not Curley.

It was hard to pin down the "why" of the hope. Boston had lost to New York just at it always had in tight situations, and it was still stuck in a divisive Irish city versus Yankee state dispute that resulted in having no winner. But if there was any way out of the "same old" situation, how would that happen? It was hard to pin down just what it would be.

The cast of characters gave few clues. Three men were running against Curley, but clearly Hynes was the main competition. John B. Hynes was from the same Irish American, city-born, Democratic Party background as James Michael Curley, and yet he wasn't Curley. It would become clear that he was a breed apart.

Some people seemed to know instinctively that it was time to do something different. They felt that the city was mired in the quicksand of stagnation and needed a change. No one could be sure that Hynes would represent or effect that change, but they could be quite sure that Curley would not. At the very least, John B. Hynes was the lesser of two evils.

The trend of the campaign was fairly predictable. Curley cited his long experience and his ability to get things done. Hynes argued that the city had become a dismal failure and urged voters to restore Boston's good name. The vote on November 8, 1949, was a large and close one. Curley got his largest vote ever, but Hynes got about twelve thousand more.

People stayed by their radios through the night listening to returns from this tight election, or they went to bed without knowing the result and awoke to find that they had a new mayor—his name was Hynes. It was startling to many, exhilarating to a few and fascinating to most. The *Boston Globe* predicted, "The decision rendered yesterday by the voters of Boston of the City of Boston, marks the end of one era and the beginning of another."

Now the question became, "Is it really the end or an era? Can it possibly mean something new?" Could Hynes actually do the things he promised or hinted at? Could he overcome the inertia, the negative feelings of malaise, the corruption and the bad reputation? Could he overcome the social and religious antagonisms that had endured for decades? Would there, *could* there, be a new Boston?

People who asked those questions were thinking the way casual observers often think. They wanted to see immediate change. The calendar had turned a page and so the city should do the same, and we should be on a new track. But that is seldom how history happens. Usually change takes time, improvements are made in starts and stops and restarts over a slow, plodding, trial-and-error path from here to there. And so it would be in 1949 and 1950 and through much of the decade. Change would come, but in measured moments. And that change would be fraught with error.

That was all ahead. But for the moment, now that Boston could catch its breath and reflect, Bostonians asked: who was this new mayor anyway? He wasn't James Michael Curley, but who was he?

Hynes was a small, fifty-three-year-old man of indifferent appearance; a neat man with rimless glasses and good manners who looked more like a banker than an Irish politician but with a background that matched those Irish politicians who had preceded him rather congruently.

Whoever he was, he was in place now. He was the new man who would have to begin to build a new Boston by restoring its reputation, its hope and its sense of direction. And in many ways, he was the "non-Curley." He looked a lot like the "acceptable" Irish politicians of yore, more in the tradition of Hugh O'Brien and Patrick Collins than Honey Fitz and James Michael.

John Hynes did not wish to rekindle class warfare or antagonize the downtown business interests. It wasn't likely that he would pit the neighborhoods against the city core or Catholics against Protestants in the combative way of Curley and—now that you mention it—Cardinal O'Connell. This, by itself, was something. But were those the only differences or was there more behind this ordinary-looking man?

# John B. Hynes and the Spirit of Change

Certainly there was another factor likely to play into the restructuring of the relationship among the people of Boston, the government and the business interests. With the death of Cardinal O'Connell in 1944, Richard J. Cushing had been named archbishop of the Boston Archdiocese. Where O'Connell had been autocratic and patrician and a leader of an almost in-your-face Catholicism, Cushing was more plebeian and approachable. But more than that, he was ecumenical before that became a popular and politically correct word.

Cushing seemed a curious candidate for this fence-mending, healing role. As a young man, Cushing had trouble deciding whether to be a politician or a priest. Always a strong speaker, he had actually campaigned on behalf of candidates, even raising money speaking from the back of a sound truck. At last feeling a strong calling, he attended St. John's Seminary in Brighton. His stentorian tones would thenceforth come from another direction.

His political background had given him useful experience. Cushing knew how to court publicity and use the media and cultivate a positive image. He was outgoing and particularly proactive in forming better relations with people of various ethnicities and religions. Cushing said he would "refrain from all arguments with our non-Catholic neighbors and from all purely defensive talk about Catholics." He was way ahead of the spirit of Vatican II, which lay a few years ahead. He promoted good fellowship by speaking to Protestant congregations and Jewish audiences.

So, in Cushing and Hynes, Boston had two people working for unity and cooperation, something it hadn't had in years from either the political or spiritual fountains of thought. For his part, the mayor called upon the downtown Republicans and consulted with business leaders on financial matters. And—here was a change—they seemed willing to confer on him the political legitimacy and cooperation they had always denied to J.M. Curley.

In a practical vein, Hynes focused first on the pressing need for low-cost housing and directed the Boston Housing Authority (BHA) to begin building housing projects. It was at this time that working-class neighborhoods like Brighton got the Fidelis Way project, a brick pile of buildings with some of them six stories in height, near the corner of Washington Street and Commonwealth Avenue and abutting St. Gabriel's. The South End got its Cathedral project, Jamaica Plain its Bromley-Heath housing, the Franklin Field housing went up in Dorchester and the huge Columbia Point housing project arose in South Boston, along with many others.

At first these projects seemed like answers to a pressing problem, and perhaps they were. Over the years, however, many became racially segregated slums themselves, socially isolated and unwelcome in the communities in which they were built. But they were welcome when they appeared, and looking back is always easier.

If this had been the extent of the mayor's attempt to make a new Boston, it would have been sadly wanting, but it was not. He would present a surprisingly wide vision, and though not much would be completed in his ten years at the helm, some things would, and important spadework loosened the soil of entrenchment for the next decade and the next mayor.

Perhaps the most significant move in this regard dealt with the Prudential Insurance Company of America, which was looking for a location in the Northeast for a large regional office. When Hynes learned about this, he at once suggested the abandoned railroad yards of the Boston & Albany Railroad that separated the Back Bay from Huntington Avenue and the South End. This was simply an opening gambit, for Hynes didn't yet have any way to make that happen, but he got the attention of Prudential, and early in the next administration the negotiations that he had begun would bear fruit.

He also went in another new direction that would ultimately pay off. He enlisted the support of the many high-powered universities in and around Boston. They had been an untapped or uncooperative resource for many years. At the outset, they offered economic reports and urban planning studies, just the kinds of things at which they had expertise beyond what city personnel or casual consultants could offer.

But all this rather amorphous and seemingly disjointed activity began to coalesce around the Boston City Seminars, a forum aimed right at the problems of the city, at a time when colleges began to express interest and responsibility for contributing solutions. These seminars were held under the aegis of Boston College and directed by the Reverend W. Seavey Joyce, S.J. and Edward J. Logue, who would head the Boston Redevelopment Authority and later pointed to these seminars as a key to bringing together the political and business communities.

Located in Chestnut Hill not far from the cardinal's residence at Lake Street and Commonwealth Avenue, Boston College had moved here from the South End, with significant building during the 1940s doubling the size of its campus. Now, under Joyce's leadership, it was casting an eye back toward Boston with these influential seminars.

At one of these in October 1954, Hynes spoke on the topic, "Boston, Whither Goest Thou?" in which he stated his belief that a coalition of business and government leaders could work together to put the city on a solid foundation economically, with an eye to clearing its slums, revitalizing its neighborhoods, rebuilding its downtown and adding a modern highway system.

With those things in hand, it could then build a Back Bay Center, a convention center, a government center and a second harbor tunnel. He took opening steps to accomplish these things, establishing an Auditorium Commission, a Government Center Commission and the Boston Redevelopment Authority (BRA), which would see to the demolition of tenement houses in the "New York Streets" area just north of Dover Street (near the present *Boston Herald*). It was called this because the streets were named for places in New York State, from Albany to the west. In this location, light industry and commerce would be built, though it would take a while to attract businesses and complete its development. The area was considered ideal for businesses because of its proximity to the railroad, Fort Point Channel and the Southeast Expressway.

Though the New York Streets project displaced some families, mostly African Americans, little was said about the human difficulties imposed on the departing residents, and little was done to help them. On the whole, the project attracted little attention and demolition was done by September 1957.

Another urban renewal project that would in time become extremely controversial, not only in Boston but also nationally, was the West End redevelopment. This area seemed to some to fit very nicely into the requirements of the U.S. Housing Act of 1949. The federal policy that evolved from this law targeted blighted urban areas. These would be removed and replaced by income-producing buildings. The federal government would pay two-thirds of the cost of buying up slum properties. The city, having bought them, would clear the land and resell it to a developer at a cut rate, who would then build new properties that would pay the city higher taxes.

The Housing Act gave the power of eminent domain to agencies of the city, in Boston's case its housing authority. The preferred areas would be near the business areas, so in this way the West End filled the bill. The planning board issued a *General Plan for Boston* in 1950 that called for the redevelopment of 2,700 acres.

The former West End was situated roughly between today's Massachusetts General Hospital and T.D. Garden, with New Sudbury Street as its eastern boundary. It was a community formed by immigrants, with as many as twenty-three thousand Italian, Jewish, Irish, Greeks, Armenians, Poles, Russians and others, mostly families. In the 1950s, the population had begun to drop.

West End, Green Street.

The area consisted of narrow, congested streets that some said looked European and might today be seen as charming. But outsiders viewed it as an impoverished slum likely at any time to be swept by fire, and they wanted it cleared. Protests were heard, but they were not well organized. Here is where the "Mahatma," Martin Lomasney, could have made a difference as a community organizer, but he was long gone and no one else filled that role, so the community was doomed. A persuasive person could have argued that this was a working-class community, much like the North End, with people who were gradually doing better economically. (In fact, a lot of the deterioration took place in the years after the redevelopment plans had been announced, not before.)

But those who favored clearance wanted this neighborhood in the inner city to be rebuilt to attract wealthier residents who would bring in more revenue. Tenants were told that suitable housing would be found for them, but in many cases this did not happen. Some were allowed to think they could move back to the area when it was finished, but that would have been a pipe dream. The old neighborhood would be gone. When new housing was built it would be beyond their reach.

The area involved was forty-six acres where 2,700 families lived. It would be replaced in part by high-rise housing in five units with 477 apartments.

# John B. Hynes and the Spirit of Change

This certainly would not accommodate all those forced to leave. Besides, the new housing would be too pricey.

A hearing was held by the BRA, and opponents gathered under the leadership of Joseph Lee, but they were too few and too late. Eviction letters went out a few months later. The BRA was using the Housing Act of 1949 to level the West End. That act gave incredible power for governments to take land, housing and even neighborhoods by eminent domain. The working-class residents and their tenements and streets would become a new neighborhood of high-rise apartments called Charles River Park, shopping centers and parking lots.

The Housing Act of 1949 that Congress had passed called for decent housing for every American family, but it didn't back that up with funding, so it became in many cases simply a license to level, and that's what happened to Boston's West End. The leveling brought some controversy at the time and a great deal in years to come. Some still recall it with bitterness. The whole thing showed great insensitivity at the least, since it was driving out poor people in favor of wealthy ones.

Class distinctions appear to be at the base of it to a large extent. Outsiders, who had never lived there, considered the West End a slum. Residents just thought of it as an ordinary neighborhood. They didn't understand why anyone would want to destroy it and were slow to realize that the bulldozers were actually coming. The city considered it blighted and in the way of progress. It even stopped providing services like garbage collection so that "blight" became a self-fulfilling prophecy.

Owners of these tenements did not get paid adequately for their properties, and many tenants had trouble finding new homes. Nearly half of the former tenants wound up in more expensive places that weren't as good as what they'd had. It was clearly a seller's market. Many reacted like refugees and displayed their grief, which is usually associated with being driven from your home and neighborhood as in a time of war.

Historic preservationists were able to save the Old West Church and the Harrison Gray Otis House, just as they would later succeed in preserving the Sears Crescent at Government Center. Those remain as a few "mementoes" of what was once an urban neighborhood.

By the summer of 1960, the West End neighborhood was cleared and it was then razed. The project was next put out to bid for redevelopment, with Jerome Rappaport the low bidder. As the plan called for, he got it at a reduced rate, but people smelled a rat because he had campaigned for Mayor Hynes as a student at Harvard in 1949, when he headed the New

Boston Committee. As it turned out, financiers did not flock to him wishing to back the project, but he finally got backing from the John Hancock Life Insurance Company, which were then in competition with Prudential and its development on the rail yards of the Back Bay.

Rappaport's architect, Victor Gruen, envisioned Charles River Park as a sort of suburb within the city. He planned five urban villages with greenery, but the place lacked the cachet he expected and did not create any enthusiasm. Moreover, the high-rise apartment buildings look more suitable to suburban Miami than to downtown Boston.

The city faced negative implications, too. The new income that eventually came had to make up for all the years the land lay empty, and that did not come easily. Moreover, its urban renewal policy received such a black eye that many future attempts would fail. Those in other parts of the city paid attention to the preemptive way the West Enders had been treated and fought hard to prevent a recurrence on their own turf.

So things were changing, but not all of the change was good. When you've been through decades of stagnation, with little new building or physical change, you're bound to have pent-up demand, and that appears to be what happened when Hynes replaced Curley and offered people a glimmer of hope.

Now things that had been proposed years earlier might be possible, and current political actions like the Housing Act of 1949 or the formation of the Boston Redevelopment Authority looked like golden doorways that might open onto the promised "New Boston." We might call it the "*At Last*! Effect."

It would be a surprise if everything done during the ten years of Hynes worked out well. Most of them didn't. Major projects brought poor results, and the fact that so many of them were crammed into a tight time frame makes them appear even worse. It seems in retrospect that the administration stumbled out of the gate, rushed around trying things out and, for the most part, botched the job. The housing projects proved ultimately to be disasters, as did the West End clearance. And then there was the Central Artery.

That was opened at the very end of John Hynes's ten-year period as mayor. A future mayor (Menino) would call it the "other Green Monster," but he was about to tear it down and he had no hand in building it, so that was easy for him to say. Even Hynes can't take the credit/blame for planning it. That began in the 1920s when traffic was bad but not yet brutal.

The original notion was to run an elevated highway between North and South Stations, but it became longer than that. The Central Artery was built through the heart of the city, and that meant that property had to be taken. About a thousand buildings had to be knocked down and nearly twenty thousand people displaced. Sections of Chinatown, the North End and the financial district had to be torn down to make room for this new road.

The fact that most of the Central Artery was elevated caused many problems by itself. Like the elevated rapid transit lines that ran at that time through Charlestown, the Sound End and Roxbury, the Artery blocked sunlight, separated parts of the city and created an eyesore in plain view that soon had most people viewing it negatively. While the Forest Hills–Everett line let riders look inside people's windows like some fast-moving Edward Hopper painting, the Artery gave drivers in stalled cars and trucks views of some fine architecture but also blocked views of the ocean from the downtown business area.

The Artery would be built in stages, beginning with the part that would run north from High and Broad Streets. The negativity of the public had a positive offshoot, however. The residents complained so much that the southern part was put underground. John A. Volpe, governor at the time, decreed that the final section, south of Congress Street, would run beneath Dewey Square in the South Station area to Kneeland Street in the Chinatown section.

Known as the Dewey Square Tunnel or South Station Tunnel, it was the widest vehicular tunnel in the world when built—six lanes. It still exists, although it has been altered. Its fumes are now ventilated, and the original tunnel now serves as the southbound lanes of Interstate 93. Most people do not recognize it and few call it by its former names.

In addition to its horrendous appearance and barrierlike functionality, the Central Artery was outmoded as a traffic route almost as soon as it was built. The intention of building intersecting arteries like I-695 (the Inner Belt) to take the load off never materialized nor did the planned Southwest Expressway that would have acted as the extension of I-95 from Canton to north of Boston.

It opened in 1956 and had far too many access points all too close to one another and was regularly tied up in traffic jams all day and part of the night. Backups going into and out of the Sumner and later the Callahan Tunnel caused constant frustration, as did the short area of the road that connected with Storrow Drive and the Mystic/Tobin Bridge. This span required crossing several lanes in a short distance to reach your exit and became another default bottleneck.

While this was being built, the Southeast Expressway was constructed between 1954 and 1959 from Massachusetts Avenue South (eventually) to Braintree. Later the Massachusetts (Mass Pike) extension was brought into

Boston in 1965 along the old B&A right of way bringing more traffic to both the Southeast Expressway and the Central Artery.

One of the positive contributions of the Hynes administration was the moving forward of the idea of a Freedom Trail. William Schofield, a *Boston Herald* editor and columnist, had the idea of making a linear and visible connection between local historical landmarks. Schofield, though familiar with Boston, had trouble finding the historic sites himself and figuring out the best way to organize a walk between them, so he sat down with Bill Winn of the Old North Church to organize a trail, and Schofield printed it in his *Boston Traveler* column.

Schofield urged the mayor or chamber of commerce to pick up on the idea before the summer, writing, "Not only would it add to the personality of the city, but also it would please the tourists." The idea pleased Hynes, and he got people right on it so that by June 1951 the plan became a reality as the Freedom Trail.

The connection between locations eventually became a red brick path between sixteen sites, two and a half miles through downtown Boston, from the Boston Common to Bunker Hill Monument. Promoting tourism was its purpose, and it did that quite well. Two years later, forty thousand people had visited the Freedom Trail. In 1974, Boston National Historical Park was established, and a visitor center on State Street gave out free maps and sold books. This was in addition to the 1966 information center on Boston Common. There was also a Freedom Trail Foundation. By that time, the number of visitors neared four million per year.

Along with Schofield and others, Mayor Hynes deserves credit for understanding that the city was one of the most historic in America and had many important historic buildings that had been preserved (though many had not). By casting a spotlight on its history, Boston had the potential to become an increasingly important tourist attraction. Schofield and Hynes deserve credit for tapping into this resource and for taking steps to make that happen. This attention to preservation would extend to other things like architectural styles and the reuse of older buildings in years to come. In many cities, when a building had outgrown its original use or was in the way of progress, it was usually torn down and forgotten. The result has been a "plain vanilla" look, of which Boston cannot be accused, except perhaps in the West End.

Boston's population hit its peak in the 1950 census with 801,000 people but then began to decline. Despite Hynes's best efforts, taxes began to rise and many middle-class people moved to the suburbs. The federal

# John B. Hynes and the Spirit of Change

Freedom Trail and Faneuil Hall.

government had unwittingly helped to accelerate suburbanization through its G.I. loan program for veterans. This allowed veterans to purchase new homes with nothing down and thirty years to pay, and it encouraged new construction, most of it in the inner suburbs, to fill the need created by the housing shortage of the middle and late 1940s. It was easy to choose a new house in a leafy suburb over an old one in the city.

Hynes, through his BRA, was able to slow the city's decline and begin its revitalization starting with the Prudential Center and auditorium/convention center and the early steps to develop a government center. In 1956, the waterfront revitalization was begun by the Massachusetts Port Authority.

Despite the decline in industry after World War II, Boston used its proximity to large universities to increase its importance in things like banking, law, medicine and later electronics. That industry spawned largely around Route 128, the circumferential highway ten to fifteen miles from the city, but Boston benefited from its presence.

At the same time that Boston was taking tottering steps toward renewal, a suburban growth spurt was occurring in a ring around Boston due in part to G.I. loans but also due to the building of the nation's first circumferential highway. Up to the 1920s, Boston had truly been the hub, with spokes radiating out as highways, many of them built before the general use of automobiles and not really suitable for what was coming. The traffic, especially in downtown, was constantly clogged, and relief was necessary. A beltway, or circumferential highway, seemed to be the answer.

The DPW (Department of Public Works) commissioner at that time was William Callahan, the person for whom the Callahan Tunnel was later named. His notion was to designate a route for traffic to bypass Boston about fifteen miles outside the city using mostly existing roads.

This was no freeway. Anyone trying to navigate it had to keep a sharp eye for black and white "128" signs that zigzagged through the outlying towns, often in heavy traffic with backups at every traffic light, especially at major intersections. Callahan added improvements to this patchwork a little at a time, but it was a bypass in name only. Something more was needed.

Callahan and the state began to plan a modern limited-access highway. This freeway-style highway would be built to replace the earlier patchwork of two-lane roads on approximately the same route. It would bear the same name and was meant to solve the same problem: too much traffic in Boston.

Route 128, Gloucester.

# John B. Hynes and the Spirit of Change

They built a little of it during the 1930s, but that was interrupted by the Second World War, and it wasn't until the late 1940s before work resumed. Much of the new road was usable in 1951. The first section that opened traced a long curve to the right from Braintree to Wellesley. At its finish in 1956, the highway inscribed an arc around Boston from Gloucester in the North to Braintree in the South. It offered an alternative to driving through Boston, but it also provided an avenue of growth for Boston industry and Greater Boston technology. It was the venue on which the newfound cooperation between academia, business and government could take place.

Even today, more than half the state's business activity takes place inside 128, and that began shortly into the 1950s. M.I.T. had been America's leading research institute in preparing for World War II and developing defense technologies. It continued that role during the cold war, while at the same time its labs hatched products and sprouted industries, and from those sprang consulting firms and startup enterprises.

The Boston-area colleges, in cooperation with Mayor Hynes, had begun during the 1950s to take an interest in local business and government. Research labs at Harvard and M.I.T. had been pioneers in newer technologies using electrical currents and magnetic fields, and the Second World War had only speeded up this development. M.I.T. in particular was instrumental in making the area a center for research and development. It was able to claim successes in such things as radar and microwave ovens, as well as air defense systems and in the early development of computer technology.

Boston and Cambridge had people with inventive minds and bright ideas, but they needed capital to make these ideas into products and systems. Boston investors now had the technology companies to invest in, so Boston provided the capital that made Route 128 the technology highway even before Silicon Valley got started.

One group that provided capital was the American Research and Development Corporation (AARD). Companies like John Hancock invested in AARD, as did M.I.T. The Bank of Boston, the area's largest bank at the time, also provided investment capital to these growing firms and other startups by becoming a small business investment company.

A key player in all of this was Vannevar Bush, dean of engineering at M.I.T. It was he who established Raytheon. That company often worked closely with M.I.T., as both played a big role in World War II. Bush came up with a plan for atomic research and was able to meet with President Franklin Delano Roosevelt. He handed FDR a one-page sheet describing his plan. Within minutes, FDR had OK'd it, and Bush went on his way to begin the

Manhattan Project, which would lead to the harnessing of atomic energy and to the atomic bomb.

When Route 128 was built, people called it "the Road to Nowhere." But the availability of large and accessible spaces a short distance from Boston and from M.I.T. and Harvard soon created a demand. Businesses, mostly manufacturing and many of these in electronics, bought land and set up shop near the new road.

By 1955, the highway became so popular that *Business Week* ran an article called "New England Highway Upsets Old Way of Life." They called Route 128 "the Magical Semicircle." It had nineteen companies with seventeen thousand workers by 1957, almost all of them from within 4.5 miles of Boston.

The plants, of course, were larger than they had been or could have become had they remained in older cities like Boston or Cambridge, and most of them were high-tech companies. Real estate developers quickly pounced on this trend and rode the wave, creating the first modern industrial parks. These were close to one another, as well as to the labs of universities. Raytheon, one of the major players, relocated in Waltham on Route 128, and other companies followed. The road and the area grew over time to become "America's Technology Highway."

# Chapter 8

## *Collins, Logue and the New Boston*

When Hynes stepped down in 1959, state Senate president John Powers—who had given him strong opposition four years earlier—was the heavy favorite to replace him. He had four opponents, Gabriel Piemonte, James Hennigan, John Collins and John McMorrow. In the September 22 primary, the voters gave Powers the most votes and John F. Collins the second most so that those two would face off in the November 3 final election.

Like Curley and Hynes, both were Irish Bostonians, and their positions on issues gave voters little to separate them. Each promised to improve the city's failing economy. They differed a great deal in image, and that would become clearer with the use of television as the election got closer.

One other difference separated them more clearly, and it would turn out to be decisive, but not in the way one might have expected. Powers had the greater political support by far. Senator John F. Kennedy, soon to be president, was in Powers's corner, as was the powerful Cardinal Richard Cushing. Powers also had the backing of most elected officials, and the city's influential labor unions were strongly behind the short and dynamic Senate leader.

Collins had served in office but had few negatives. A few years prior he had contracted polio and now used a wheelchair. He came across on television as an open-faced, pleasant and sincere fellow. So he had the markings of an underdog. Powers, by contrast, seemed tough and political.

Collins realized these things and also understood that the strength of his opponent was also his weakness. John Collins was exactly the kind of candidate who could use Powers's great strength against him, as one might in a martial arts contest. He kept jabbing away at Powers's political support, making it clear that Powers was a political insider and not someone who would give them the newness they wanted. He cleverly asked the public to "Stop Power Politics."

At the end of October, a news story came out that seemed made to order for Collins's message. It seemed to capture in a capsule what he'd been saying all along. The police had staged a raid on a gambling house that made the front pages. It had a news photograph of the place where the raid took place clearly showing a Powers campaign poster. Right along Collins had been talking about Powers's political connections and hinting that some of them were shady. This photo seemed to back that up.

Shortly afterward, Collins appeared on a television show and used the opportunity to draw a clear distinction for the voters. He looked into the camera and told them, "Except for you, I am alone."

He wasn't alone on election day. The voters were with him, and he prevailed by a crushing twenty-four thousand votes, an outcome that was perhaps the most stunning in Boston electoral history. Though Powers was quite different from James Michael Curley, he seemed to have inherited some of the antimachine sentiment that had elected Hynes three times and now favored Collins.

Collins set out to do what he had envisioned. If Curley was ethnocentric and lacked vision, and if Hynes made several stabs at change and progress without fully developing them, then John F. Collins—Boston's new mayor in 1960—was a decided visionary with a precise idea of how to get started.

Hynes had broken the logjam of ethnic strife and made peace with the business community. Those things had made a difference. He had taken steps toward rebuilding, some of them disappointing, and he'd left a number of ideas or projects unfinished.

But even though Hynes had established better relationships with the private sector, the city remained depressed and still in a downward projection. Its downtown still evoked the London of Dickens. The tax rate had risen to $101.00 from the $56.80 per thousand it had been when Hynes entered office. Boston's municipal bonds were rated by Moody's Investment Service as lower than most other major cities. Business leaders had even prepared to back them up in case of an economic collapse.

Now Collins, in cooperation with Edward Logue, would take the major steps toward building a new Boston. Logue was perhaps the best-known person in the country connected to urban renewal. He had gained national prominence from his work in New Haven with Mayor Richard Lee. Logue was the man Collins wanted, and he was willing to offer a salary higher than his own to bring him to Boston. They had a meeting of the minds and then they set out to let people know what they had in mind.

On September 22, 1960, Collins and Logue announced a "Ninety Million Dollar Development Program for Boston," saying that decay was sapping Boston's greatness. This plan would be heavy on urban renewal. They wanted to get rid of the shabbiness and replace it with new income-producing properties both residential and commercial. They designated ten areas for development. Three were downtown and seven in the neighborhoods. These would ultimately involve half the people and a quarter of the land in the city. It would cost less in the 1960s because the federal government was ready to help cities with things like that at that time.

Logue was counting on getting federal aid for this urban renewal program. But the city, through the BRA with his leadership, would plan and direct the development.

For his part, Collins would work with the business community through a group called "the Vault," named for the place they met within the building of the Boston Safe Deposit and Trust Company. They met every other week, the businesses were able to offer Collins expertise and advice and they even lent the city personnel skilled in specialized areas like tax assessment, which had been a sore point for so long.

Logue was made administrator of the BRA, first on a trial basis and then permanently. He gained more federal funding, putting Boston in fourth place in the United States for federal funds received. He got state aid, too, since Massachusetts agreed to split the cost of renewal with the city. The Collins/Logue partnership made it all work. Logue was able to hire and fire, and he brought in talented people with expertise in the many areas where it was needed.

Perhaps fittingly, or even understandably, Ed Logue was a World War II bombardier and knew a lot about leveling cities. He would get a lot of that done in Boston, too.

Logue and Collins had their list of ideas they wanted to work on, but sequence was important. Unfinished business must come before new business. They still had the unfinished work of the previous administration to take care of. That meant the Prudential Center, most of all, as well as a new convention hall and the Government Center—all downtown projects.

Although costs of new development were higher than planned and work took longer, the desire for rebuilding Boston seemed to take hold and gain support. In 1964, Logue was able to revise Boston's zoning code, something that had always been under the authority of the state. The new code did away with height restrictions and would allow the city to build up with office towers that would give Boston a new skyline.

The Prudential Center had been started and then it had stalled for a significant reason. Mayor Hynes's notion of attracting Prudential to Boston by offering tax incentives had been struck down by the Supreme Judicial Court as unconstitutional. That meant that a new arrangement that would satisfy Prudential had to be devised, and it had to pass legal muster, too.

At the same time, the Massachusetts Turnpike Authority (MTA) wanted to extend the turnpike from Weston into Boston alongside the Boston and Albany rail line. Using the rail yards for the Prudential Center appeared to be at odds with this other important goal, but after some time this was worked out. Engineering studies were developed for both. Then the legal problems facing the Prudential had to be worked out.

Meanwhile, the rail yards—ready for development—contained the steel that would one day rise as the Prudential Tower. It lay there rusting for more than a year, a symbol of the stalled status of the project, while the state legislature debated the law that would let it go forward.

Major legislation made it happen. Logue's idea was to treat it as an urban renewal project. In September 1960, Chapter 121A of the General Laws of Massachusetts was used to give the Prudential tax concessions. It also abolished the City Planning Board and gave its powers to the BRA. The BRA declared the rail yard area blighted and stated that the Prudential Center would benefit the community. These two factors made it eligible for funding.

The Prudential resumed construction in March 1962 on what would be a fifty-two-story building, the tallest in Boston at the time, followed by other buildings, while the turnpike extension was built along the northern edge of the yards and next to the tracks still used by the railroad.

Earlier in that year, the long-planned Boston Common Underground Garage was completed amid public charges of corruption and graft. It gave three levels of new parking to the downtown area without building another eyesore of a public garage above ground.

By mid-decade, the Prudential Center and the extension of the Massachusetts Turnpike were about complete, as was another tall building, the State Street Bank and Trust Company's headquarters on High Street, which led to buildings by other banks like Shawmut, Bank of Boston and Bank of New England. The Government Center and Atlantic Avenue Project were also on their way.

# Collins, Logue and the New Boston

Prudential Center.

The Government Center project was different from the West End project and didn't run into the same problems. Scollay Square, which it replaced, was not a neighborhood in the usual sense. It was a place people came to often during hours of darkness, and when it came time to demolish it, while some regretted its passing, few people came forward to actively defend it. Buildings would be razed and people displaced, but not on the scale of the West End.

The project stirred a lot of interest. Boston was actually going to put up some significant buildings, which, along with the Prudential Center, were going to change the way the city looked. They would also change how people felt about Boston. The malaise of the '40s and '50s still hung over the city like a pall, but the new development would help to lift that.

Boston needed a lift. One of the country's top developers of urban real estate had been asked at that time what he would do to improve Boston. William Zeckendorf said, "The first thing I'd do is tear the whole goddamn place down." He might have been joined by enthusiastic pilers-on and those who did tear down a sizable part of it. But the early years of Collins-Logue also offered hope. There was a "Spirit of the New Boston."

A snowball effect led from one project to the next and a feeling among private developers that they should join in this boom that had been generated by public planning and public spirit. If this was where Boston was headed, they wanted to be on board.

The Government Center would be built in the area where Scollay Square had been. That area was close to downtown, beginning where Tremont, Cambridge and Court Streets meet and going east to Congress Street and north to Sudbury Street. The selection of Scollay Square for a government building was an idea that had been around for a while, but it had a new importance as part of a plan to rejuvenate Boston. Scollay Square represented what can become of a long-neglected area, which it became during the first half of the century and the long Curley years.

Logue, in fact, said "a rundown skid row, predominantly nonresidential, was a perfect vehicle to undertake a traditional clearance and redevelopment project." He might have added that the federal government would have no problem in declaring it a slum, even though it was dear to the hearts of its patrons and even provoked nostalgia among its older "alumni."

Though some would recall fond memories of the area, its seediness had become even more noticeable in recent years; when it was slated for demolition, most Bostonians did not resist. The project gained federal approval and funding in 1958.

The best-known building in Scollay Square was the 115-year-old Quincy granite "Old Howard" Athenaeum, the bawdy burlesque house that had known so many different entertainment types over its years—from Junius Booth to Buster Keaton to Rocky Marciano to Jerry Lewis, to name a few. Most recently it featured strip shows; those had led to its closing by city order in 1953. When, in June 1961, it had a suspicious fire, the city tore it down before it could be rebuilt, driving a stake into the heart of those who had set out to restore it.

It would take three years to raze all the buildings on twenty-two streets. All except one, that is. The Sears Crescent, an 1816 building, was saved largely through the efforts of one man. George Gloss, owner of the Brattle Book Shop, organized historians and book lovers to try to save the city's historical book center on Cornhill. It was the site of many used bookstores where people would go to pore through musty tomes on dusty shelves in search of literary treasures.

The street ran in a curve that matched the curve of the red brick Sears Crescent. Gloss cited customers as far back as Ben Franklin and argued that the buildings should be saved, especially the Sears Crescent. It was, but the rest were not. Sears Crescent, a historic red brick building of five stories,

# Collins, Logue and the New Boston

Scollay Square.

brought with it a sense of "pentimento" of the recently erased Cornhill, a street that traced the same curve as the current building. Cornhill (and Brattle Street) were the locale of ancient bookstores so loved by browsers.

In keeping with its preservation of the past, Sears Crescent housed the U.S. Figure Skating's World Museum and Hall of Fame, as well as its national headquarters and, on the outside of its first-floor corner establishment, the 1837 steaming kettle, also the world's largest. (The shop is now a Starbucks.)

Sears Crescent anchored one end of the center. Far to the north would rise a completely different style of building. The U.S. General Services Administration (GSA) had plans to put its new building in the Back Bay, about where the Hancock Tower stands today. But Congressman John W. McCormick talked them into building in the new Government Center instead (as the city wished). The large, hook-shaped building stands today on New Chardon Street.

Also on that north side of the plaza would rise the double-towered John F. Kennedy Federal Building. There were also two Suffolk County courthouses adjacent, as well as two office buildings that belonged to the state (Saltonstall and McCormack), a huge parking garage and a kiosk that marked the T station below, made famous by the 1950 Kingston Trio song known as "Charlie on the MTA," in which Charlie is doomed to ride forever because

Cornhill with Sears Crescent.

he doesn't have the exit fare. It is this Charlie whose name graces today's passes known as "Charley Cards."

In time, a crescent-shaped building of three sections would stand on Cambridge Street across the plaza from City Hall. Known as 1, 2 and 3 Center Plaza, its graceful curve follows the street and approaches the oppositely curving Sears Crescent at the Court Street intersection.

Government Center also has City Hall Plaza and the City Hall. The architectural firm of I.M. Pei and Associates was hired to plan the new plaza. It consulted with historian Walter Muir Whitehill, and the plans were ready in 1963. The federal government had already approved the land taking ahead of time, which was unprecedented. A national design contest was held for the new City Hall. That building would dominate the area, though prior to the contest the look of the building was unknown.

The contest was won by a new architectural firm, Kallman, McKinnell and Knowles. The winning design created a lot of dissatisfaction when it was unveiled, and it still does. City Hall is the dominant feature of the plaza. It is an enormous, imposing and overwhelmingly concrete structure in the style known as brutalist that was popular at that time but which many felt did not fit the Boston milieu. When the model was unveiled at the Museum of Fine Arts, it was disdained by many. One wag said it looked like "the crate Faneuil Hall came in."

Many architects like the design of City Hall but few admire the plaza. Dubbed a "brick desert," the open, windswept and sun-drenched mall was laid out between the inverted pyramid City Hall and Cambridge Street; it was dramatic in its difference from old Scollay Square. It is still thought to be impractical and hard to use for events. It has had useful purposes, however, having served as a locus for three victory celebrations for the Patriots, two by the Red Sox and one by the Celtics.

However, when Government Center is viewed through a 1960s lens when newness was desirable, and when considered for its practicality, it filled the bill. It certainly was a departure from the red brick or granite of the earlier-built parts of the city, and it also brought together all forms of government in one convenient area. It has city, state, federal and county buildings, and government is the region's major employer—nowhere more so than in Boston. So bringing them together makes sense.

Whatever a person's view of all this was, it decidedly spoke of newness in keeping with the notion of a new Boston. The groundbreaking started in

Government Center, City Hall Plaza.

September 1963, and Mayor Collins was able to occupy his office at City Hall in 1968 just before his time in office expired. He used it even though the building was unheated, since he wanted to complete his term in the new building. (A future mayor—Menino—proposed in 2008 moving city government to a different area and selling the land.)

The excitement caused by all this new building in the public sector led to a similar spurt among private investors, especially insurance companies, banks and law firms. There was also the War Memorial Auditorium adjacent to the Prudential Center, which would also have a new Sheraton Hotel. Behind that, on Huntington Avenue, the First Church of Christ Scientist extended its complex in 1963 with BRA help, adding buildings, apartments and a reflecting pool seven hundred feet in length.

In the Chinatown–South Cove area, Tufts–New England Medical Center established itself in several rehabilitated buildings in the area where it had begun as the Boston Dispensary. It made it part of its mission to treat those in the local community as well as outsiders. Its doctors are also members of the faculty of Tufts Medical School.

This building by private enterprise would lead to the construction of the John Hancock's sixty-story tower near Copley Square, which would be the city's tallest building when completed in 1976. Its glass façade carried the reflection of nearby Trinity Church, thereby depicting the new Boston and the old.

Downtown Crossing also got some attention during this period in cooperation with the Central Business District Committee. Victor Gruen, who had planned Charles River Park, was hired as an advisor, and he suggested street closings to create an area something like a mall. Those changes were actually made in the mid-'70s.

While the old Boston seemed to have been shunted aside when Government Center made its splashy debut, this wasn't entirely true. The mayor's office at the new City Hall gave him views of the old Boston including Faneuil Hall and Quincy Market with food trucks unloading their wares and litter behind the food markets, as well as the waterfront with its occluded views of the harbor.

# Chapter 9

# *Urban Renewal and Historic Preservation*

The BRA also had plans for renewing some of the neighborhoods. It had spent time and money on the downtown and would spend more, but it wanted to upgrade the neighborhoods and make them into newer income-producing areas with an improved housing stock. It would quickly find out that this would be harder in some places than others.

It was hard for the most part because people still had memories of the way the West End neighborhood had been treated. Some neighborhoods were now organized and on the watch for BRA interventions. The BRA members knew that neighborhoods that were represented on the City Council would be troublesome for them. So the North End and South and East Boston would oppose any attempts at urban renewal and would make such a loud stirring that other neighborhoods, which might be more docile, would then be alerted.

So they wouldn't go there. But even so, they underestimated the resistance they would find. Neither Charlestown nor Allston-Brighton had representation on the nine-member City Council, so they looked like easy pickings. But they certainly would not be pushovers. Residents of these districts didn't want their houses torn down whether they were shabby or not, and they didn't want to have them displaced by new housing that would be too costly for them. They organized for political action.

During this same period, the state of Massachusetts also ran into resistance in its attempt to build a Southwest Corridor through Hyde Park, Jamaica Plain and Roxbury. The displacement this would take drew a lot of protest, as did the plan to build an Inner Belt across Boston, Brookline, Cambridge and

Somerville. Governor Francis Sargent declared a moratorium on highway building inside Route 128 in 1970, and plans for the Inner Belt (Route 695) were dropped the next year. Community protests were gaining strength and could point to successes. This was one of those periods in our history when a great many people, particularly poorer people, were distrustful of their government—in this case, city and state government.

They had reason for distrust. Edward Logue had used the right words in trying to get past the remnants of the West End debacle. He said that the BRA wanted to include community groups in the planning for renewal. He called it "planning with people." But it seemed he wanted to decide for himself which people he would include in the planning, and they would be mostly people who would support the changes BRA wanted.

The Washington Park Urban Renewal Plan ran into this problem. It was proposed in 1963 for the Roxbury neighborhood. This project actually did try to involve the people of a neighborhood, but not all the people or most of them. This was a five-hundred-acre site that had gone from 70 percent white to 70 percent black in the recent decade. The project emphasized rehabilitation and "planning with people." But the planning was done with certain people of the community. Members of Freedom House, a community organization, worked with the BRA on what would become middle-class housing in what had been a working-class area. Those left out of the planning phase were offended and said so.

This was the most extensive residential urban renewal project of the 1960s, and it emphasized rehabilitation rather than clearance, so Logue had reason to be confident when he staked his reputation on it. However, many lower-class people felt that this was not a community-driven project. They also said that it would be hard for them to find new places to live because of two factors: a shortage of low-cost housing and racial discrimination. Logue, at one point, told the City Council that he did not see that it was the BRA's responsibility to find replacement housing for people who were forced to move. The council, however, disagreed, and put a hold on future land taking until that was resolved.

Another area where Logue and the BRA took two steps forward and one step back was Charlestown. This was another blighted area that Collins and Logue targeted for renewal. Property values had plunged there, and people were moving to the suburbs at a rapid rate. The BRA planned to rehabilitate an incredible 90 percent of the homes there, but this was too much for the "townies." They'd had a bad history with government coming into their community and imposing its plans. At the turn of the century, the Boston

Elevated Railway had built its platform for overhead trains right up Main Street, blighting that route for most of the century.

Then in the 1940s, a city housing project had taken more homes and left Charlestown with unwelcome low-income housing. Then, a decade later, ramps had been built for the Mystic-Tobin Bridge near City Square, taking still more homes and leaving an obliterated view, blocked by massive steel pillars. It was a small wonder that the BRA met strong resistance.

Public meetings became rowdy and even violent. Monsignor Lally of the BRA was taunted and heckled when he tried to speak, and the pastor of a local church was punched when trying to espouse the BRA plan at a local hearing. The major plan was doomed. Logue only salvaged a modicum of success when he was willing to cut way back on what would be done and promised to remove the elevated trains from Main Street. (This was a promise kept. It came down in 1975.)

North Harvard Street in north Allston at the intersection with Western Avenue, not far from Harvard Stadium, was commonly known as "Barry's Corner." It became another bone of contention in the early 1960s. The insensitivity shown to West End residents was repeated here. Fifty-two buildings housing seventy-one families were to be demolished in favor of a high-rise apartment building that would cost $4.5 million of mostly federal taxpayers' money and bring in ten times the tax revenue. The building would have 372 luxury units.

The homes were private property, and their owners were informed of this plan on the evening TV news. The BRA said that every effort was being made to find housing for those who would be displaced. The BRA took a full year before holding a public hearing in front of a boisterous crowd that saw this in terms of class warfare—taking from the poor and giving to the rich and using tax money to do it.

The residents appealed to every possible source, but these appeals fell on deaf ears. Still, they managed to delay the project, and after four years, the BRA suspended demolition and appointed a commission to study the situation. Among this panel's findings was a recommendation to give the owners back their titles if they would agree to rehabilitate their houses in accordance with BRA standards. Sadly, this was ignored.

It took a horde of policemen to break up the crowd of protesters as the final houses were taken over and then demolished in October 1969. A development finally was placed there in the 1970s that had mixed-income housing.

The whole thing was a public relations nightmare for Logue and for the BRA. He had articulated the goal of planning with people and did talk to community groups. But neither he nor the BRA could overcome the perhaps impossible task of satisfying the residents of poor neighborhoods who didn't want their houses or homes taken from them. That kind of thing would be difficult at any time, but during the period of student and neighborhood uprisings and protests, it brought a particular bitterness.

# THE WATERFRONT

The waterfront would be the next important project. Atlantic Avenue in the post–World War II era had rows of shabby buildings, rotting wharves and little-used docks. Most people paid little attention to the waterfront. Its proud past was behind it. It had long been decrepit and forgotten. The fishing industry had largely removed to South Boston, so there wasn't much activity to be seen on a regular basis in the area. If it were ever to have a resurgence, that would take leadership.

The elevated portion of the Central Artery loomed between this coastal area and the downtown, only adding to its isolation and neglect. In fact, the dilapidated condition of that area had made the land cheap when it came time to build that highway. Like a depressed area that was easy to bulldoze, the waterfront could be eclipsed without much ado. No wonder Boston lacked vitality. Even the downtown was pretty much empty on weekends. People had no reason to go there. A new Boston would have to revitalize these areas, too.

But that was what urban renewal was supposed to do—revitalize an area. It hadn't done that in the West End, that was true, and the Central Artery wasn't much to look at, but perhaps this would be different. The BRA took over the project, got some federal money and encouraged private development as well.

The first work in this area was the erection of the modernist-style Waterfront Towers on India Wharf, designed by I.M. Pei in the 1960s and completed in 1971. The wharf had been designed by famed Boston architect Charles Bulfinch, as were numerous structures in the waterfront district. It was a deepwater wharf that had been used for ships that brought cargo to and from China and India. Pei's design presented a complete departure from the brick and granite that were Bulfinch's media of choice, and Pei's massive concrete was a chasm away from the traditions of built Boston.

At the time of their building, the two forty-story apartment buildings were surrounded mostly by parking lots, which were bountiful and scattered

Harbor Towers.

throughout the district. So these isolated towers stood out and also offered spectacular views. Priced at the time as affordable, they also offered a way to bring residents close to the financial district, which usually was deserted except during weekday business hours. Since one of the goals of redevelopment was to attract middle-income people to the city, this was at least a start. As the waterfront project brought other structures, the towers seemed less objectionable to look at and more desirable to live in.

Edward Logue, sensitive to the criticism that followed the West End project, called attention to the change in approach from what had been done with that part of the city. In Harbor Towers, he said, "nothing is being displaced but the fish, and we're preparing an aquarium for them next door." And so they were, and Central Wharf would be the location for the New England Aquarium in 1969. There is no record that the fish ever complained.

The rest of the development would not use modernist buildings. In fact, to a large extent, the planners tried to use existing historic buildings in new ways, thus building this part of the city within its largely federalist framework. This was no easy task, and some of it took more than a decade to complete, but its ultimate success gave Boston its distinctive look that has so much appeal for tourists.

Historic rebuilding looked like such a natural solution when it was completed (especially in contrast to the modernist renewal areas) that one has to reflect for a moment to realize that it was a new concept in its day. But once Boston had shown the way, other cities rushed to copy it.

But in the 1960s, much of Boston still looked as tired as the waterfront. Even the downtown had been hit by the loss of manufacturing and the loss of people to the suburbs. Growth was stagnant. Boston had gotten national attention from its bold attempts at urban renewal, but the results didn't please most Bostonians. That was especially true of those who had been evicted from the "renewed" areas. But in other areas, too, like the North End, community groups had formed to protect their neighborhoods from similar treatment.

Collins and Logue's "Ninety Million Dollar Development Program for Boston" had three downtown projects on the slate. One of them called for rehabilitating this downtown waterfront and Faneuil Hall district.

The BRA hired Kevin Lynch and John Myer of M.I.T. in July 1961 as consultants. Their charge was to come up with an urban renewal study and a plan for improving the blighted waterfront as well as people's perception of downtown Boston. They produced a plan in just eleven months for what became a very successful redevelopment, except that it would take much longer than expected.

They were dealing with an area where marine trade was largely gone, replaced to a large extent by wholesale food dealers and warehousing or storage functions. Few people lived there, and few came there except for these functions. Lynch and Myer would have to suggest ways to add vitality not only to this district but, by transfer, to the city itself.

It may have occurred to the developers that people would be attracted to the area if they were able to recall the historic marine functions that had served the area in the past. That could be done by the refurbishing of the buildings of Bulfinch and others. It would be a happy result if the people who would be interested in such an area were the very ones who came to the district. In any case, it worked out that way.

The Downtown Waterfront–Faneuil Hall Renewal Plan listed six broad objectives that gave the planners a framework over which to drape their goals:

1) open the city to the sea;
2) reinforce the neighboring districts;
3) preserve historic buildings and traditions;

4) create a waterfront residential community;

5) increase visitor traffic to the city; and

6) strengthen the city's economy.

They might have added a seventh, which was to become implicit in the development. The redevelopment of the Faneuil Hall–Quincy Market complex became part of the project as early as 1964 but was not begun until many years later.

Opening the city to the sea was a big charge, and we'll deal with it separately. Reconnecting the city with the waterfront was a desirable end that would have to deal with the Central Artery, which essentially acted as a barrier to that connection. However, they were able to mitigate its imposing presence by relocating two of the ramps, one at State Street, not far from the Custom House Tower, and the other at South Market Street, just beyond Quincy Market. The two ramps had been close together, and the relocation at least made an opening. Atlantic Avenue was also moved inland with an eye to allowing more open space along the harbor.

Later, the Christopher Columbus Waterfront Park would be built in this area with public funds, but in the years just before it was built, the area had tin warehouses and chain link fences that kept the public at bay. The BRA envisioned a "walk to the sea" from the Government Center. Sasaki Associates, which had designed Copley Square, was given the job, and it really did consult with citizens as it did its planning.

The firm was expert in grading filled-in land, which this was, having once been part of the harbor. In 1976, huge crowds gathered in this open area to watch the "Tall Ships" in the harbor during the nation's bicentennial celebration. When people saw the new park, they asked themselves (and the authorities) why the whole waterfront couldn't be open like this. This became the plan for a harbor walk.

The park was built essentially opposite the 1826 Quincy Market so that pedestrians could walk from City Hall, through the soon-to-be-redeveloped marketplace, cross a relocated Atlantic Avenue, enjoy ocean views and watch marine activity in the new park that recalls Boston's long maritime history as well.

Another refurbished area that gave marine views would be Long Wharf with its new, large hotel and docks for hydrofoils and other boats on the park side. It is also between Long Wharf and Central Wharf, site of the New England Aquarium.

Part of reconnecting with the waterfront would come simply by allowing more direct public access. While twenty-first-century visitors would find that they could view the ocean from nearly any of the wharves, this was not the case as this project began. Piece by piece it would happen.

The walk to the sea and its associated reconstruction brought value to housing that would gradually be added to the area, and those who would live in the new units tended to be the middle- and upper-income people whom planners hoped for. That was because housing with waterfront access and ocean views that was also near downtown was prime real estate and therefore expensive. The new housing that would be added was, in many cases, located on rebuilt wharves, in refurbished warehouses or other buildings of historic interest.

Extending waterfront access north from Long Wharf also brought the active waterfront closer to the North End, just as the walk to the sea brought it closer to downtown, thus meeting those goals.

Using historical buildings, such as those associated with the maritime past, was a way of following a historical model. This was certainly true of the saving of the Faneuil Hall–Quincy Market iconic district, and this was probably the first major project that used this plan. This model was just then coming to the fore, largely as a result of the writings of Kevin Lynch, the M.I.T. designer of the project, in his work *The Image of the City* and Jane Jacobs, who wrote *Death and Life of Great American Cities.* Both espoused changing from the modernism that was being used everywhere and turning to plans based on building cities to a human scale.

Lynch pointed to landmarks like Faneuil Hall as essential components in building an image of cities like Boston. Edward Logue understood the need for preservation of these building, too. It is no surprise then that the team decided to preserve these buildings, which had been slated for demolition. Lynch and Myer's model celebrates Boston's past by saving its important buildings. Their ideas were not accepted right away, and it took fifteen years to get financial support to complete the Faneuil Hall Marketplace renewal. But once it had been done, other cities jumped to imitate it while Bostonians asked themselves, "What took so long?"

Two political changes helped to get the historic development model going. One was the National Historic Preservation Act, passed by Congress in 1966. It set up a federal program for preserving and protecting historic buildings and was right in line with what the Boston planners were thinking. Using a valuable building in a new way was just what they intended to do, and it was another idea that began in Boston at this time. This alone was a long way from the stagnation that got this project in motion to start with.

Boston also had a change in administration in 1968 when John Collins retired and Kevin White was elected mayor. White was very dynamic and prodevelopment. Edward Logue had also left his job as BRA director to run, unsuccessfully, for mayor. In his place, White appointed Robert F. Kenney to work on the Faneuil Hall redevelopment.

But Kevin White wanted to run things himself. He often overrode Kenney's decisions and finally brought city planning into his own office. Planning of the neighborhoods went into a new city department he created for that purpose. At the same time, the real estate market of the 1970s had the effect of making the private sector the most important in new initiatives.

## FANEUIL HALL MARKETPLACE

The brilliance of the renewal effort in Boston can be seen most clearly in the saving and refurbishing of Faneuil Hall Marketplace, a complex consisting of Quincy Market, the North and South Market buildings and Faneuil Hall.

Quincy Market.

It was the single element of the waterfront plan that would show the way to other developers who wanted to use Boston's exceptional history and what remained of its historic infrastructure to make it a top tourist destination, It also bolstered Boston tourism as a newly thriving service industry, which had replaced the manufacturing industries that had been lost. Some of this achievement was not among the original goals, but it fell into line quite nicely.

Let's see how that happened.

During the Hynes administration, Quincy Market existed primarily as a wholesale trading center behind Faneuil Hall, an area used especially for food products. It was shoddy, outdated even for that use, and the area was often clogged with traffic. Plans were already in motion for a new produce center to be built in South Boston. (Such a center would later be built near the Southeast Expressway.) As for the future of Faneuil Hall and the market buildings, their future was gloomy, their further existence questionable. Demolition was certainly a possibility, but after some previous urban renewal forays had been less than satisfactory, a new way of doing things might have a chance.

It was only in 1963 when the waterfront was being developed and Edward Logue, director of the BRA during the administration of John Collins, decided that the historic market must be preserved. At that point, he wasn't sure how to make that happen. The interest in saving this area was a departure for Logue and a new way of thinking for the BRA that seemed, to many people, to bulldoze first and ask questions later. The marketplace would turn out to be a slow, deliberate development that blossomed into an outstanding reuse and spread the message nationwide that preservation and reuse were not only possible but advisable.

The redevelopment of the Market complex began in 1964 as part of the Boston Redevelopment Authority's Waterfront Urban Renewal project. With city renewal funds and a $2 million HUD grant, the BRA acquired the needed buildings, relocated the food wholesalers, installed new utilities throughout the six-acre area and restored the exterior façades.

In 1966, the U.S. Congress passed the National Historic Preservation Act, and straightaway a proposal was made to the BRA by Benjamin Thompson, architect. It called for holding on to the three Parris-designed market buildings and turning them into an urban marketplace. The BRA followed up on this proposal by applying for a Historical Preservation grant from the U.S. Department of Housing and Urban Development.

Boston got a $2 million grant in 1969 based on a report about Faneuil Hall that was submitted by Architectural Heritage and the Society for the Preservation of New England Antiquities. The grant would be used for the cost of restoring the building. The following year the BRA bid on 6.5 acres that included the three market buildings.

The BRA took control of that area in 1970, a downtown plot on which stood the three market buildings and Faneuil Hall, located between the market buildings and Congress Street at the back of City Hall. The market buildings were Quincy Market in the center with its copper dome in the middle part of the long building, and the North Market and South Market buildings, which flanked it on either side. All were nineteenth-century buildings designed by architect Alexander Parris and built under the leadership and vision of Mayor Josiah Quincy. They are granite, Greek Revival–style buildings, and when they were built, they were one of the largest urban developments in the country.

Faneuil Hall had been built as a market through the donation of Peter Faneuil in 1742 and had been added to by architect Charles Bulfinch. It stands in Dock Square with a statue of Samuel Adams in front. The project would require restoring not only the buildings but also the streets, and while the historic aspects would be preserved, especially the architecture, it was meant to function as a contemporary shopping and recreation area. This idea was new, and no one knew for sure that it could be done.

In June 1971, Benjamin Thompson & Associates was named as designer. However, the developers it chose did not meet the construction schedule, and another had to be chosen. A plan that was given the BRA's approval did not pass muster with the mayor. Kevin White liked the idea proposed by the partnership of Thompson with Jim Rouse to develop the area while maintaining its historic aspects. Their unique vision of an urban marketplace appealed to him, and they were promised a tax reduction.

The Thompson-Rouse project had some of those same overtones. At a time when American cities were withering, Thompson said his vision was to "reassert the values of urban life and to preserve urban quality, vitality, and beauty on a human scale."

However, Thompson-Rouse found it difficult to raise the funds for the project, and nothing was done for three years. Ironically, financial support came about when Chase-Manhattan Bank agreed to put up half the money if Boston-based banks would provide the rest. White put the pressure on and the local banks also came through.

Rouse wanted the marketplace to open on the 150th anniversary of the original opening, August 26, 1976, and he intended it to be a marketplace, not a shopping center. It was to be a place where local small capitalists could sell their wares.

The Thompson team of architects wanted to retain the Greek Revival style while incorporating modern elements such as lighting and furnishings. This was no historic restoration. It was a series of new facilities placed within historic buildings, their patina showing through in the granite walls, rough wooden beams and brick interiors without taking away from their modern uses.

The team wanted to use local businesses and make streets that would be easy and interesting for pedestrians to navigate as they shopped. It introduced pushcarts as a novel way to introduce startup businesses. They, along with the open market stalls and the many food choices, spoke of revitalization and had just that effect.

However, when looking for financial support, the project ran into skeptics who doubted it could succeed without an anchor department store. Such stores had been contacted, but the space wasn't right for them and the place was too dingy and old for stores that liked to be bright and new.

On opening day, Quincy Market had a lot of empty, unrented space—about half of it—so they filled it with pushcarts of merchandise, much of it made by artists and craftsmen. Even then, employees of the architectural firm and of the developer had to man some of the pushcarts. So, opening day was filled with doubts.

It needn't have been. The forty-three pushcarts gave the aura of a festival to the building, and although crowds for the opening ceremony were modest, by noon employees of Boston businesses came to see for themselves, spent the lunch hour there and told their friends and colleagues about it. The crowds grew and grew as the day went on, and during the first three days, 150,000 visited the marketplace.

They found that all their senses were engaged. They encountered buildings from their historic past, quality goods and foods of restaurant quality, as well as the scents of coffee beans, baking bread, grilling sausages and other familiar and exotic flavors. They would not trip over shopping carts and have their ears blasted by canned music. Both were banned.

In time the marketplace also drew people to the waterfront, which was adjacent, and it drew tourists—lots of them. By 1980, the number of tourists visiting Boston had doubled from what it had been before the marketplace opened. At 15 million a year, it was outdrawing Disneyland. As Thompson had predicted, the anchor was the city itself, and it was the novelty of the experience that drew people in and brought them back. They called it a "festival marketplace."

# Urban Renewal and Historic Preservation

The tourism phenomenon was a surprise. They had expected mostly local people to come. However, this influx of tourists may have led to the diminution in the number of local merchants and the rise in the number of chains.

The marketplace was opened in three phases, starting, as mentioned, with Quincy Market in 1976, followed by the South Market building the following spring and the North Market building the year after that.

Quincy Market's three floors and seventy-five thousand square feet were used as a food market with many restaurants, delicatessens, cafés and other food outlets with merchandise from many countries. In the center, a rotunda was created by making a hole in the ceiling that revealed the dome. In the space beneath that, they placed pushcarts and stands at the outset. Later, lunch tables were set up as a place to sit down while consuming purchases. The building had old trade signs placed near the ceiling in this area.

During the second phase, the streets next to North and South markets had to be paved (using brick, cobblestone and granite) and landscaped. These were closed to traffic and used for vendors, arts and crafts areas and seating. In time, promotions and live entertainment were held in the space between Quincy Market and Faneuil Hall. This included magicians and jugglers, clowns and musicians.

The South and North Market buildings developed during the second and third phases were leased for retail and office use, three floors including the basement. Several of these shops were and are quite distinctive and sell things not found elsewhere. They also have restaurants. However, the potential value of the spaces attracted larger stores of the chain variety, which was not the original intent. This became increasingly evident when the office spaces attracted wealthy clients.

Architect Benjamin Thompson had the idea of building glass canopies out to the sides of Quincy Market, giving it considerably more rental space. A new greenhouse north of Faneuil Hall was also built.

Not only did the marketplace spark interest in other cities, it also generated excitement for both historic preservation and the construction of new buildings in its own city. This was truly the cornerstone of the new Boston.

From there, Boston went on to rebuild its business district, adding a shopping area at Copley Place, revitalize the harbor and improve access to the airport and travel through the center with its Big Dig. All of that came in the following four decades as Boston rose from its dinginess to become a great city.

# Bibliography

Abbott, Katherine M. *Old Paths and Legends of New England Border*. New York: Putnam's, 1907.

Aliosi, James A., Jr. *The Big Dig*. Beverly, MA: Commonwealth Editions, 2004.

Allen, David Grayson. *The Olmsted National Historic Site and the Growth of Historic Landscape Preservation*. Boston: Northeastern University Press, 2007.

Allison, Robert J. *A Short History of Boston*. Beverly, MA: Commonwealth Editions, 2004.

Beatty, Jack. *The Rascal King*. Reading, MA: Addison-Wesley, 1992.

Bulger, William M. *James Michael Curley: A Short Biography with Personal Reminiscences*. Beverly, MA: Commonwealth Editions, 2009.

Cudahy, Brian J. *Change at Park Street Under*. Brattleboro, VT: Greene Press, 1972.

Curley, James M. *I'd Do It Again*. Englewood Cliffs, NJ: Prentice-Hall, 1957.

Curtis, John Gould. *History of the Town of Brookline*. Boston: Houghton-Mifflin, 1933.

Dennehy, John W. *A History of Brookline, Massachusetts: From the First Settlement of Muddy River Until the Present Time*. Brookline, MA: Brookline Press, 1906.

Dineen, Joseph F. *The Purple Shamrock*. New York: Norton, 1949.

Edel, Matthew. *Shaky Palaces*. New York: Columbia University Press, 1984.

Hardwicke, Greer, and Roger Reed. *Images of America: Brookline*. Dover, NH: Arcadia, 1998.

Hepburn, Andrew. *Biography of a City: Boston*. New York: Scholastic, 1966.

Holloran, Michael. *Boston's "Changeful Times": Origins of Planning and Preservation in America*. Baltimore, MD: Johns Hopkins University, 1998.

Holmes, Alexander S. *Boston: The Growth of a City*. Edison, NJ: Chartwell Books, 2007.

Howard, Brett. *Boston: A Social History*. New York: Hawthorn Books, 1976.

Kennedy, Lawrence. *Planning the City Upon a Hill: Boston Since 1630*. Amherst: University of Massachusetts Press, 1992.

Kennedy, Patrick L. *Boston Then and Now*. Thunder Bay, ON: Thunder Bay Press, 2010.

Marchione, William P. *Images of America: Allston-Brighton*. Dover, NH: Arcadia, 1966.

O'Connor, Edwin. *The Last Hurrah*. Boston: Little-Brown, 1956.

O'Connor, Thomas H. *The Athens of America: Boston 1825–1845*. Boston: University of Massachusetts Press, 2006.

———. *Building the New Boston*. Boston: Northeastern University Press, 1993.

———. *The Hub*. Boston: Northeastern University Press, 2001.

Puleo, Stephen. *A City So Grand: Boston 1850–1900*. Boston: Beacon Press, 2010.

Rosegrant, Susan. *Route 128*. New York: Basic Books, 1992.

Schorow, Stephanie. *Boston on Fire*. Beverly, MA: Commonwealth Editions, 2003.

Shand-Tucci, Douglass. *Built in Boston*. Amherst: University of Massachusetts Press, 1999.

Van Hoffman, Alexander. *John F. Kennedy Birthplace*. National Park Service, U.S. Department of the Interior, 2004.

Warner, Sam Bass, Jr. *Streetcar Suburbs: The Process of Growth in Boston 1870–1900*. Cambridge, MA: Harvard University Press, 1962.

Writers' Program (Massachusetts). *Boston Looks Seaward: The Story of the Port, 1630–1940*. New York: AMS Press, 1975.

# Note from the Author

As a boy and then an adolescent, I lived on Commonwealth Avenue in Allston in one of those newly built apartment buildings that sprouted up after the trolley tracks were laid. Those trolleys ran outside my front window, and even as a four-year-old, I was fascinated by all the people and activity for which they were a focal point. From my third-floor window, I had a window on the world.

My school was near Union Square Allston, part of the auto mile, a busy and exciting thoroughfare—busy with streetcars as well as cars. As a boy, I delivered newspapers with routes in the Aberdeen section of Brighton and along Beacon Street between Cleveland Circle and Washington Square.

When I became old enough to drive, I delivered newspapers throughout Brighton, and I remember being impressed by all the Catholic institutions on the hilltops. When I was still quite young, a friend asked me to stand with him along Commonwealth Avenue to watch the funeral procession for Cardinal O'Connell. My memory is of huge, silent crowds and a long caravan of cars.

I rode trolleys and trains all over Boston and, as a boy, took the railroad to a place called Riverside in Newton. I also rode my bike everywhere, including onto the newly paved Route 128 when it was about to open.

For a while we lived on Corey Hill, and I could walk to college from there, down Summit Avenue to Coolidge Corner and then through the Longwood area to the Fenway. From the windows of our apartment we had a good view of the Boston skyline. At that time the only tall buildings were the Custom House and the old John Hancock Building. It was a skyline destined to rise, but we didn't know that at the time. I was still living there when they began to build the Prudential Center, and not long afterward, the city became more vibrant.

By that time I was teaching in Brighton in a school near the seminary and not far from Brighton Center, and one year my students made a mural of cutout black paper against a light blue background that represented the skyline of the new Boston. Here, at last, were those new buildings and that new spirit.